THE COMPLETE GUIDE TO INVESTING IN GOLD AND PRECIOUS METALS:

HOW TO EARN HIGH RATES OF RETURN — SAFELY

BY ALAN NORTHCOTT

THE COMPLETE GUIDE TO INVESTING IN GOLD AND PRECIOUS METALS: HOW TO EARN HIGH RATES OF RETURN — SAFELY

Library of Congress Cataloging-in-Publication Data

Northcott, Alan, 1951-
  The complete guide to investing in gold and precious metals : how to earn high rates of return safely / by Alan Northcott.
      p. cm.
  Includes bibliographical references and index.
  ISBN-13: 978-1-60138-292-4 (alk. paper)
  ISBN-10: 1-60138-292-8 (alk. paper)
  1. Gold--Purchasing. 2. Precious metals. 3. Metals as an investment. 4. Investments. I. Title.
  HG293.N67 2010
  332.63'28--dc22
                                    2009053980

PROJECT MANAGER: Nicole Orr • PEER REVIEWER: Marilee Griffin
INTERIOR DESIGN: Samantha Martin • PRODUCTION DESIGN: Holly Marie Gibbs
FRONT COVER DESIGN: Meg Buchner • meg@megbuchner.com
BACK COVER DESIGN: Jackie Miller • millerjackiej@gmail.com

Printed on Recycled Paper

Printed in the United States

We recently lost our beloved pet "Bear," who was not only our best and dearest friend but also the "Vice President of Sunshine" here at Atlantic Publishing. He did not receive a salary but worked tirelessly 24 hours a day to please his parents. Bear was a rescue dog that turned around and showered myself, my wife, Sherri, his grandparents Jean, Bob, and Nancy, and every person and animal he met (maybe not rabbits) with friendship and love. He made a lot of people smile every day.

We wanted you to know that a portion of the profits of this book will be donated to The Humane Society of the United States. *–Douglas & Sherri Brown*

The human-animal bond is as old as human history. We cherish our animal companions for their unconditional affection and acceptance. We feel a thrill when we glimpse wild creatures in their natural habitat or in our own backyard.

Unfortunately, the human-animal bond has at times been weakened. Humans have exploited some animal species to the point of extinction.

The Humane Society of the United States makes a difference in the lives of animals here at home and worldwide. The HSUS is dedicated to creating a world where our relationship with animals is guided by compassion. We seek a truly humane society in which animals are respected for their intrinsic value, and where the human-animal bond is strong.

Want to help animals? We have plenty of suggestions. Adopt a pet from a local shelter, join The Humane Society and be a part of our work to help companion animals and wildlife. You will be funding our educational, legislative, investigative and outreach projects in the U.S. and across the globe.

Or perhaps you'd like to make a memorial donation in honor of a pet, friend or relative? You can through our Kindred Spirits program. And if you'd like to contribute in a more structured way, our Planned Giving Office has suggestions about estate planning, annuities, and even gifts of stock that avoid capital gains taxes.

Maybe you have land that you would like to preserve as a lasting habitat for wildlife. Our Wildlife Land Trust can help you. Perhaps the land you want to share is a backyard—that's enough. Our Urban Wildlife Sanctuary Program will show you how to create a habitat for your wild neighbors.

So you see, it's easy to help animals. And The HSUS is here to help.

2100 L Street NW • Washington, DC 20037 • 202-452-1100
www.hsus.org

TRADEMARK STATEMENT

DEDICATION

Dedicated to my beautiful wife, Liz, my constant companion
through life's adventures and strength for more than 30 years.

With special thanks to Nicole Orr at Atlantic Publishing,
my editor, and to Doug Brown, publisher,
who shares my love of and concern for animals.

TABLE OF CONTENTS

Chapter 7: Finding a Broker   157

Chapter 8: The Other One   181

INTRODUCTION

You are probably reading this book because you believe there may be good reason to invest in gold, particularly because of turmoil in the financial markets. You want to see if that is true, and what methods of investing are best. Fortunately, you will find those answers in this book, including discussion of the different opinions about where the price of gold is headed, and the pros and cons of the great variety of ways that you can take a financial interest in it.

There are many people saying that the best time to invest in gold and precious metals is when the economy seems to be taking a turn for the worse — and the more inflation seems to dominate our lives, the more people are looking for a constant, such as gold, to stabilize their sense of lasting wealth in their savings. Apart from the monetary side of owning gold, there is also the delight of owning jewelry, and decorative gold has always been recognized as a status symbol. It seems inevitable that currency will become more worthless, given the amount of money that is being "invented" in 2008 and 2009 by the government to fend off a financial crisis. In 2008, there was a total of $829 billion of U.S. currency in circulation, most of which was held outside of the United States. By 2009, the amount of currency in circulation increased to $890 billion, a trending growth that leads investors to believe that a greater amount of money in circulation will be chasing ostensibly the same number of goods and services, resulting in an increase in prices, too.

But this view is simplistic, as it does not account for many other economic factors, such as whether savings increase, so that the money is not spent on services. While these finer points may be debated at length, most people would agree that the dramatic increase in available currency must translate to inflationary pressure from the government and the creation of what could be excess currency.

Many people think gold has always increased in value in the long-term; however, this may not be the case. Even though the value of gold remains the same because it is immutable, does not corrode, and does not really change over the centuries, the value of everything else is decreasing. So, therefore, you need many more dollars to buy the same piece of gold. Certainly, gold shows a steady increase in price over time, and with the recent amount of spending by the government, it seems this trend is bound to continue.

Although gold is the focus of this book, it also considers other precious metals, as the arguments that apply to investing in gold can be related to similar investments such as silver.

Gold and other precious metals have stood the test of time, and have often been turned to for stability when society has faced an upheaval. Gold has long been recognized as a store of wealth, the ownership of which allows you to shrug off the changes of the current financial system and ensures lasting value in your portfolio. The metal, however, is so much more than an IOU, which is all any paper currency can be seen as with the abolition of the gold standard in the twentieth century. Because paper currency lacks the intrinsic value it once had when it was backed by gold until the 1970s, the exchange of money simply takes the form of a promissory note, as many see no limits to the Federal Reserve's increase in currency production. Gold, on the other hand, maintains its value, but there are some considerations that you need to be aware of because although the long-term ownership of gold has always proved successful, there have been market fluctuations that have been disappointing to some buyers.

In 2009, gold broke the thousand-dollar-per-ounce barrier, and there are good indications that it may rise higher — perhaps a lot higher. Owning gold as a metal has some disadvantages, including storage and security, as well as the absence of any income until you sell. There are other methods with advantages and disadvantages that you can use to profit from an increase in gold's price, and those are thoroughly dissected throughout this book. Financial instruments related to gold can benefit from any increase in its price and can also provide a regular income. Note that just because a security is related to gold does not mean that it will inevitably increase in value as gold becomes more sought after, and the reasons for this are covered in depth so that you will be able to decide on the wisest investments for your situation.

CHAPTER ONE

Why Invest in Gold?

Why should investing in gold be regarded as one of the smartest moves the average investor can make in a hard economy? The old advice of practicing diversification in your portfolio has usually included buying some gold or precious metals, perhaps up to 10 percent of your portfolio in various forms. However, the advice of many analysts is for significantly more than this amount to be placed in a financial instrument related to the price of gold.

Diversification is usually considered the wisest course of action, even though it will never result in the highest returns. By its nature, diversification — investing in many different types of financial securities and deposits — cannot give the maximum return on investment because you are putting your money in a variety of different investment vehicles that are subject to different performance levels. Obviously, you can only achieve a maximum return if you selected the one type of financial instrument that would go on to perform the best. The reason for diversification, however, is if your selection is not optimal and you make an investment in something that loses money, then you only lose a proportion of your portfolio because your money is spread around in several different investments. On the other hand, if you do not diversify your investment portfolio and instead invest in the highest-performing vehicle, you risk losing all of your money instead of just some of it.

With the state of the financial markets in 2008 and 2009, it is difficult for even the best of analysts to know with any confidence which companies or shares are going to perform well in the future. Long-term investment suffered a severe blow by the machinations of the market, and it does not seem that the current financial climate favors the perennial wisdom of "buy-and-hold." Those who follow the stock market in the short term can see opportunities, but it is a sad fact that the majority of would-be traders — at least 80 percent — lose money and give up in the first six months of their trading career.

Real estate, which was believed for many years to be unshakable as an investment that would always increase in value, has let many people down with a thump, and it will take several years for the housing market to get back to a place where the buying and selling of houses is anything other than a trial. Although fortunes can be made by opportunists taking advantage of irrational or erratic markets, it takes knowledge, skill, experience, and perhaps a little luck to stand a chance of profit in such circumstances.

An investment in a savings account or certificate of deposit does not attract the return needed to even keep up with published inflation figures, and changes the way these are calculated, meaning that your actual requirement for increased spending to maintain your standard of living is much higher than the published numbers. To estimate your return on your investments, use the calculator at **www.bankrate.com/calculators/retirement/roi-calculator.aspx**. This calculator allows you to fill in the appropriate fields about your savings method, then choose whether you want to see the results adjusted for inflation.

For those who find these investments and markets too risky and difficult to fathom, there is one store of value that has demonstrated, over the centuries, an ability to maintain its spending power — gold. Both new and experienced investors can be assured that gold is a reasonably safe way to hold on to their savings and maintain their value. Gold has consistently been used as a medium of exchange for both goods and work since ancient times and has not suffered devaluation in the same way as paper currency. *Learn more about its history in Chapter Two.*

One reason for this is that there is only a limited amount of gold in the world, and the amount mined each year is also restricted by physical constraints. Gold and other natural resources benefit from the economist's simple principle of supply and demand, where a limited supply ensures that the value is maintained.

History has demonstrated time and again that paper currency, with its intrinsic ability to be manipulated by governments when times are tough, is almost bound to cause inflation from overproduction and lose its value. It is almost too simple to point to examples of this in your own lifetime — for instance, how much was your first automobile, and what would it cost to buy a similar vehicle now?

In fact, the principle of supply and demand operates to increase the price of gold and precious metals any time that the stock market starts to behave badly. Savvy investors put their money into gold as a safety move if they believe that the stock market may be a risky place for their portfolio. Thus, a shaky stock market almost guarantees an increase in the gold price by increasing the demand. Weakness of the dollar is the other factor in the equation. If the dollar was considered to be strong, investors might choose to stay in cash and cash equivalent financial assets. With the weakness evident from 2009, there seems to be no better place to invest than in gold and gold-related financial instruments, further pushing up the demand. In fact, sources like the *Wall Street Journal* and MSN Money reported gold as being at its peak in 2009. According to MSN Money, gold neared $1,100 an ounce in the early days of November that year.

This deduction, although valid, might suggest to some skeptics that the price of gold was being pushed artificially high by emotional trading, and that if and when the stock market appeared to be stable again, the price would go down as investors sold gold and bought into stocks and shares again. While there may be an element of truth in this accounting for short-term fluctuations in gold price, there are deeper underlying reasons that gold is well-positioned to continue increasing in cost.

For much of the twentieth century, the United States appeared to be prospering with a thriving economy that was the envy of many other nations. Stock prices showed strong growth, and the strength and lasting power of the dollar was evidenced by the fact that commodities around the world were priced in terms of the dollar. It was indeed considered the "golden" currency.

Underneath all of this, the government has been adopting an unsound and cavalier attitude toward the currency, generating more paper dollars whenever they were needed in order to stimulate the economy. Who can ever forget the speech of Ben Bernanke, then-governor of the Federal Reserve Board, when in 2002 he spoke of dropping dollar notes from a helicopter in order to keep the economy going? Accordingly, he was appointed as the successor to the Federal Reserve Chairman Alan Greenspan in 2005.

A student of the Great Depression, Bernanke chose to answer to the defeating deflation by simply issuing more money, and he noted that creating inflation by doing so was in the government's interest, reducing the real value of the government debt. Unfortunately, as one-time presidential candidate Ron Paul has pointed out, the continuing inflation from unnecessary growth in the money supply causes an "inflation tax," which is hidden taxation on everybody because of the falling value of each dollar.

There have been reasons for the dramatic growth in the money supply, most notably the events of September 11, 2001, which shook confidence in the apparent robustness of the financial sector, and the "bailouts," such as that of Lehman Brothers in September 2008 to avoid an immediate crisis in the markets from the failure of a "too big to fail" company. For some, to blame these events on only inflation would be to deny the continuing economic policy that has increased the national debt of the United States consistently for several decades.

Government sources reveal that the debt was a mere $370 billion in 1970, increasing to $907 billion in 1980. By 1982, the debt was more than $1 trillion, more than $3 trillion in 1990, $5 trillion in 2000, and hit double-figures in the trillions in 2008. This is money that is owed currently, and the amount is much larger when you take into account the government commitments to programs such as social security, Medicaid, and Medicare, which will require payments in the future. The debt is typically financed by sales of Treasury bonds, and China and Japan are the chief bondholders, meaning that the two countries play a role in financing the U.S. debt. This is not surprising when you realize how many dollars they earn from exporting to the United States. In 2004 alone, China was expected to make more than $150 billion from exporting goods to the United States.

This issuing or creating of more dollars to finance existing commitments, including interest payments on existent debt, fuels inflation and devalues any dollars that are held in any accounts.

Although it is not unusual for a civilization to go down this path, currency seldom starts out on this track. Paper banknotes are easier to carry and use than gold bars, so what is called "fiat currency," or money declared legal by a government, usually starts out as an IOU for gold or silver that is in storage in a bank. When there is a crisis that requires greater spending than the value of the metal held, governments succumb to the temptation to print more money than is backed by the precious metal deposits. Until that time, the value of money remains constant in terms of its buying power.

World War I required significant military spending, and this was achieved by printing money that was not covered by the reserves of gold that were held, thus suspending the gold standard so it did not hinder the war effort. Some say that this printing of money and granting of credit not backed by reserves contributed to the stock market crash of 1929. A consequence was the confiscation of gold and a revaluation to bring it in line with the amount of currency in circulation. *In Chapter Two, you will read how the gold standard was abandoned completely in the '70s.* This incident led to a bull market — in other words, a rising price of gold — for about 20 years. This truly was a demand-led increase, caused by people questioning the value of banknotes that were not securely backed by gold. These people wanted to protect their interests. It resulted in a high price that could not be sustained, and has only in recent years been achieved again.

As mentioned, real estate has not proved to be the secure investment that common knowledge would have it known as. The real estate boom, where rising prices seemed to confirm this view, came crashing down, and one of the chief causes must be recognized as easy credit; in other words, more created currency. Consider this — a bank does not have to hold all of its deposits in its vaults, but it must have a certain percentage in reserve, perhaps 10 percent, called its "capitalization." They are allowed to lend out the other 90 percent, which is backed by the Federal

Reserve System. If lending happens freely, money is being "created." For example, cash on hand of $5,000 may allow a bank to lend $50,000 on mortgage. Where did the extra $45,000 come from? It came from the fact that the bank has created the transaction. The system relies on the fact that all depositors do not want their money repaid at the same time, and in fact, such a "run on the bank" is guaranteed to cause difficulties; in the United States, it will cause the Federal Deposit Insurance Corporation (FDIC) to step in to make sure that investors do not lose. In theory, the amount lent is — in the case of mortgages — covered by the equity of the home, but this theory can fail when lending is too liberal. In other words, lending more for a mortgage than what the home is valued at results in liberal lending. Thus, such lenient policies for lending can contribute, and even cause, a bank's failure, resulting in financial hardship for the bank's customers and the community the bank is in.

In any time of financial difficulty, it is plainly obvious that the shrewd investor will look for a secure place to invest, and gold and other precious metals are clearly better than most, if not all, alternatives. The essence of their value is that they have intrinsic worth and do not depend on any government or third party standing behind them. The only question that you may be asking yourself is this: What proportion of my portfolio should be invested in gold?

THE RISKS

Having said that, as with many other desirable transactions, there are dangers to be faced and the risk of a loss. There are many dishonest people only too ready to jump on a trend and operate a scam to separate you from your hard-earned money. The common ways in which this is done are outlined in the following chapters, appropriate to the type of investment.

These are not the only risks involved with investing heavily in gold; it has been found lawful for the U.S. government to insist on confiscation, as was the case in 1933, when President Franklin D. Roosevelt prohibited U.S. citizens from owning more than $100 worth of gold coins. Those U.S. citizens who had more than this amount were forced to sell their "excess" gold to the government. *This incident is explained further in Chapter Two.* The fact is that the government only received a proportion of the amount of gold known to exist, thus a great many people did not surrender their holdings as directed. This is little consolation to a law-abiding citizen who would not want to risk being found to have broken the law.

While we cannot predict what the government will do some years hence, you should at least be aware of and guard against being scammed by opportunistic operators, and this book will guide you through the safe practices.

CHAPTER TWO

Gold's Record

ANCIENT TIMES

The origins of using gold and silver as media of exchange and for bartering goods and services are shrouded in history. It was undoubtedly scarcity and convenience that determined what elements should be used in establishing value. It would be no good, for instance, to have sand or rocks recognized as currency, as this was freely available to everyone who could take time to collect it. Therefore, sand and rocks would have been of little worth.

Before currency or coinage was invented, bartering would have been the only fair way to obtain items that you wanted from someone else. Although stealing and plundering were options, when people started to establish civilizations, the peaceful alternative of swapping one cow for ten goats, or a chicken for a sack of potatoes, would have appealed as a more sustainable form of trade.

Studies of ancient civilizations show that gold and silver have been used as convenient bartering elements for nearly 5,000 years. Originally, the metals would have been used mainly as an intermediary device. In the example above, the seller of the cow might accept a certain size of golden nugget for the animal, and in a later transaction receive ten goats for the gold. Using precious metals in this way meant that you did not have to find a trading partner who required what you had in exchange for what you wanted. You were free to take the gold to someone else who had the goods you desired. It was also easier to store value for use at a later time. In a sense, gold and silver were used as IOUs but maintained a universal value based on the characteristics of the metals themselves.

In addition to the scarcity of gold and silver, which translates into value in a small amount, gold's many properties made it the best choice for this purpose. It is durable and does not corrode. It is malleable, which means it can be easily shaped as desired and worn as jewelry, showing off the owner's wealth and providing a decorative status symbol. It is resistant and imperishable, and the majority of the gold that has ever been mined and found in the world is still in existence.

Though bartering is an option and is still used sometimes today, trading goods with a known and measurable value makes the process easier. It was in Lydia, now a part of Turkey, that the idea of making a standard size and weight of coins was developed around 680 BC. This enabled trade to be carried on much more simply, and it facilitated the buying and selling of goods and services. Modern-day bartering is much the same; instead of working in your industry for a paycheck, your compensation may be in the form of trade. For example, a freelance journalist who writes articles for a magazine may receive gift certificates from the magazine's advertisers as a form of payment rather than receiving monetary compensation.

But it was the Greeks who really embraced the idea of bartering with precious metals and developed their currency. In Athens, the Greeks established the world's first known democracy. They had a free market system and a tax system that allowed public works, such as the Parthenon, to be built and created. The Greeks are considered to have had one of the greatest civilizations of all time, and some blame their movement away from the gold standard for Greece's collapse.

Athens flourished for some time, using a monetary system based on gold and silver coinage. But they became involved in a war that depleted their wealth, so after 22 years, they came up with an ingenious method to continue funding the conflict. They discovered that if they mixed copper with gold in equal parts in their coins, they would have twice as much money. This was the earliest recorded instance of deficit spending — a situation familiar to present-day economists that occurs when more funds, or goods, are used to make purchases than are received through revenue.

Before this dilution of the currency, gold had always had a value in and of itself, and was merely cast into a convenient form for trade when it was made into coins. Everything had a price, which could be stated in terms of the weight of gold or silver required for its purchase. Essentially, the heavier the gold or silver was, the more value it was believed to have. For the first time in history, the Athenians had invented a currency that was not worth its content. The war was quickly lost, and Athens succumbed to becoming a province of the Roman Empire.

The Roman Empire lasted for many centuries, but it took no lesson from the fall of Athens. The Romans progressively debased their currency, clipping the edges of coins as a tax when entering government buildings, and mixing baser metals — such as copper with gold — for their coins. They even re-minted the same coins with a higher face value than the one inscribed in order to fund government spending. Combined, all of these practices led to the devaluation of a currency and a system that was previously strong.

The result of this was that inflation raged, and in an effort to control this by mandate, Diocletian, the Roman Emperor often noted for laying the groundwork of the second Roman Empire, issued an Edict of Maximum Prices in 301 AD. This imposed the death penalty for selling goods at a higher price than the government mandated and also dictated a wage freeze. Neither of these restrictions had any effect on increasing prices. In desperation, Diocletian dramatically increased government spending by employing far more soldiers and increasing public works. This is funded by a diluted currency, with coins simply minted from base metal with little inherent value.

This massive example of deficit spending resulted in the first recorded instance of hyperinflation. A pound of gold was worth 50,000 denari, a Roman coin, when the edict was issued, and 50 years later cost 2.12 billion denari — more than 40,000 times as much. Again, spending — unaccompanied by fiscal responsibility — played a role in the downfall of a civilization, and gold had proved its worth where currency had failed. As nineteenth century philosopher George Santayana put it, "Those who cannot remember the past are condemned to repeat it."

THE EARLY TWENTIETH CENTURY

There are many more examples of this pattern throughout history. In summary, the pattern involves firstly a sovereign state with perfectly good money, backed by gold or silver, if not by coins actually made of those metals. As society continues, there is economic development that adds public works expenditures, much like the Parthenon was built in Greece, and there are social programs that require further expenditure. Eventually, a point is reached where political factors require military expenditure to preserve its sovereignty.

Even then, the situation may be sustainable. The factor that causes the government to spend more than it has is usually war, and the unrestrained expenditure that must be made in the interests of maintaining its independence and self-government, as well as in fighting other countries. This may occur during a war, such as in the cases of Athens and Rome, or may even be at the outbreak of the war, as with what happened during World War I.

The increased amount of currency in circulation to pay for these programs (currency that is not backed by any physical wealth such as gold) causes rapid inflation and a loss of faith in the currency by the general population. As more money is chasing largely the same amount of physical goods, it is inevitable that the price of these goods increases to combat inflation, barring exceptional circumstances. As the general populace come to re-alize what is happening, there is a massive move away from the currency, which in effect collapses into physical goods, of which gold and silver are good examples of enduring value. An indirect result of inflation can be seen through the rising price of certain goods, like movie theater tickets. In the 1920s, movie tickets were sold for around $4, but saw continual increases due to inflation. By 2009, movie tickets were being sold for well over $10 in most areas of the country, hindering many people from going to the movies.

Reviewing the period up to the outbreak of World War I in 1914, the majority of the developed world had a gold standard, which meant their currencies, like the dollar or the peso, were fixed to a certain amount of gold — and also, by extension, fixed to each other. For instance, the peso was traded at fixed amount of gold, making, for example, 100 pesos equal to 1 ounce of gold. Likewise, the same amount of gold was fixed at $10, making the peso and the dollar fixed to each other. Exchange rates between currencies were established, and commerce could rely on this stability. It is interesting to note that on average, in this situation, there is no price inflation. Although it is incredible to those who are living now, inflation is not inevitable — and the gold standard meant that it did not occur, as gold was synonymous with money.

As this appears to be a remarkable statement, it is worth consider-ing the facts. If the currency is backed by gold, gold is stable and relatively constant in amount because not much of it is mined each year. Therefore, the amount of currency available is relative-ly constant. All currency in circulation has actual gold or silver in the Treasury that supports its value; so, for every dollar bill, there is the equivalent of gold or silver. This way, the currency is just a representation (or an IOU) for that precious metal in a form that is easier to carry and use during day-to-day transactions.

Now, there can be an economic boom in the country, which means that the people buy more goods, including imports, which are goods brought into one country from another. To pay for them, gold will flow away from the country receiving the goods to the countries that provide the imports. With enforcement of a gold standard, this means that the amount of currency in circulation will contract because there is less gold in the country receiving the imports to back the currency. For example, in 2005, the United States imported $14,724,672,000 in beverages and tobacco from other countries. If the United States were to pay the countries it receives the beverages and tobacco from in gold, then it would consequently have less gold in the country to back the gold standard, assuming the country were on it. Thus, an exchange of gold for imports, like this one, means that there will be less money available to back the gold standard, forcing the economy to slow down and imports to possibly fall.

As less money is being spent, prices will drop a little in the country where the goods are being made, making the products more attractive to foreign buyers. This would increase exports — goods produced in one country and shipped out and sold to another — and create a net flow of gold back into the country. And so the cycle will repeat within a narrow range, self-regulating to maintain equilibrium. Prices will never move far from their median value because of this cycle.

With the advent of World War I, the requirement for military spending meant that currency was created for which there was no gold in store. This started in Europe, as the United States did not enter the war immediately. As a major supplier of equipment to other nations in the war, the U.S. in fact received a great deal of gold in those first years from the European Allies. When the Allies could not pay in gold, the United States extended them credit. Even so, the spending required after the U.S. involvement meant that the national debt increased to more than $25 billion by the end of the war.

The governments of the world sincerely wanted to return to the stability that they enjoyed under the gold standard, which they lost when they inflated their currency supplies beyond the reserves they held, often as a result of wartime spending. But to return to a true gold standard, they would need to devalue their currency so that the amount of money in circulation matched the gold they had in store, and this was not acceptable to them. Therefore, they worked together to create what was called a gold exchange standard.

After the war, the United States held most of the world's gold, for reasons explained above. For their part, the Allies had significant holdings in U.S. dollars, resulting from the war loans that the States had made. The gold exchange standard specified that the dollar and the British pound could be used as currency reserves by other countries, and that only these two currencies would be directly redeemable in gold. This allowed foreign countries to use dollars in place of gold as the reserve of value, which would back their currency — a pseudo-gold standard relying on, and assuming, inherent value in U.S. dollars and British pounds. This was the start of a house of cards that has been collapsing — and still is. It also provides a very good reason for making sure that you have gold — something of real value — in your portfolio.

You may think that the current system — where foreign currency is backed by dollars and the dollars can be exchanged for the gold that backs them — is fairly solid, and gets around the fact that there is not enough gold in the world to back each currency individually. Unfortunately, it is really not possible to cheat the system indefinitely, and this is what the world banks were trying to do with this action.

To understand just how far the financial experts had stretched the system, revisit the year 1913, when the Federal Reserve Act was passed by Congress. It is not widely understood that the Federal Reserve is not a government agency, but rather a privately owned bank, or in fact 12 regional banks — a decentralized central bank. They are not quoted on the stock market because they are privately owned, but there are shareholders, and they are paid dividends. It is the Federal Reserve that makes currency for the United States, not Congress or any other government body. The government trusts the Federal Reserve Bank to act in the best interests of the economy.

With remarkable insight, in the discussion on the Federal Reserve Act in 1913, Senator Henry Cabot Lodge Sr., stated "The [Federal Reserve] bill as it stands seems to me to open the way to a vast inflation of the currency...I do not like to think that any law can be passed that will make it possible to submerge the gold standard in a flood of irredeemable paper currency." The inflation that he predicted has been continuing ever since.

As the Federal Reserve Bank has created and lent every dollar to the government since 1913, on all of which the government owes interest, it appears inevitable that the debt can never be repaid. It may not be a coincidence that in the same year, income tax was created. Prior to this, there were sufficient revenues from tariffs and excise tax, a tax that is imposed on certain goods or services, for the government to operate.

As previously mentioned, banks operate on a principle called fractional reserve banking, which means that they do not need to have cash on hand to sufficiently cover the deposits that they hold. The capitalization may be as little as 10 percent of the deposit. Under the 1913 Act, the Federal Reserve Bank was to keep a 40 percent reserve of gold against the currency created.

Consider now the pyramiding effect of all this fractional reserve banking. If the Feds have $100 of gold in reserve, they can put $250 into circulation. The bank that receives this can create a loan for $2,250, for a total of $2,500, backed only by $100 worth of gold, or 10 percent of the deposit from the Federal Reserve. The gold exchange standard made this worse, as the foreign central banks could back their currency with dollars instead of with gold. The same $100 of gold, creating $250 in a foreign central bank's reserve, would allow them to issue $625 worth of currency to a local bank, which could be used for a total loan of $6,250. In reality, there is less than 2 percent of real value in gold supporting that loan.

With the benefit of hindsight, it is easy to see where all this easy lending was headed, and a massive credit expansion created an economic boom, which was enjoyed by many during the

Roaring Twenties. When difficulties came along in 1929, there was no foundation to prevent a massive stock market crash and subsequent depression. The house of cards tumbled, and many banks collapsed.

In 1933, Franklin D. Roosevelt was inaugurated as President and took some drastic steps to change the situation. In particular, he required U.S. citizens to turn over gold in exchange for Federal Reserve bank notes, the so-called "confiscation," which to this day is discussed as an example of excessive intervention of government in the affairs of its citizens. In 1934, Roosevelt revalued gold from $20.67 an ounce to $35 per ounce. Those law-abiding citizens who had turned in their gold were the ones who suffered the most, and those who have kept hold of their gold realized nearly 70 percent profit.

The end result of this was the temporary establishment of some stability. These numbers were not selected from thin air, but chosen because after the revaluation, the amount of gold held in the U.S. Treasury exactly matched the monetary base — which meant that every dollar in circulation was fully backed by the gold stored. While great for the stability of the U.S. dollar, at least at the time, it also meant that every dollar in circulation was instantly worth about 40 percent less in real terms and in purchasing power.

WORLD WAR II

Because of this devaluation, exports increased, resulting in a trade surplus and more gold flowing into the U.S. reserves. This effect was increased as the threat of war in Europe caused many factories to be turned over to making military supplies, which meant that everyday items were exported to Europe, thus more gold was being received by the U.S. This served to lift the U.S. out of its depression, and meant that the Federal Reserves held most of the gold in the world. It appeared that the U.S. economy was buoyant again, and it must be said that the U.S. survived relatively unscathed from the war, in contrast to Europe, where many factories were destroyed and lives were ruined.

Once again, the war had upset the currency systems, and stability was threatened. Europe had little gold left, and the monetary system was once again in ruins. An agreement — known as the Bretton Woods agreement after the place in New Hampshire where the meeting was held — was made in 1944. This required foreign currencies to be pegged to the U.S. dollar, and only the dollar would be redeemable in gold, at a rate of $35 per ounce. To gain a little perspective, as of November 2009, gold was hovering around $1,138 per ounce, according to reports from the *Wall Street Journal*. Thus, while having gold redeemable at $35 per ounce seemed to make paper currencies stable again, the value was small in comparison to how the metal's worth has increased in the twenty-first century.

Furthermore, creating a more standard currency in the U.S. meant that the reservations of currencies in foreign countries were also based on the U.S. dollar, and thus only indirectly based on gold. This is to overlook an obvious flaw in the system, which was that the U.S. was not held accountable for the amount of gold reserves it had in comparison to the currency issued. In other words, the U.S. was not limited or restricted from printing as many dollars as it wanted.

THE VIETNAM ERA

The Vietnam War was funded and fought with deficit spending. The Bretton Woods agreement permitted this, and as many dollars as necessary could be printed to pay for the war. Any idea of a gold standard, where value in gold should be held in the Treasury to back the currency, appeared to have been totally abandoned.

Part of the Bretton Woods agreement required participating countries to sell gold into the markets to keep the price at $35. In 1965, the President of France, Charles de Gaulle, attacked the dollar standard, cashing in dollars in return for gold, and calling for a return to the gold standard. With the devaluation of the British pound in 1967, there was a run on gold and the agreement was abandoned, leaving the United States with less than half the gold reserves they had a few years before because the dollars had been "cashed in" for gold.

President Richard Nixon formally ended the arrangement, started by the French president, to convert dollars into gold on demand in 1971, with the result that all currency values became free-floating and market-driven. All currencies were now fiat currencies, valued only by the good standing of the governments behind them, and not from any reserves of true value. Because the U.S. dollar is at the center of international trade, America possesses a unique advantage over any other country in the world. The U.S. can invent as much currency as it wishes, which allows running the unbelievable deficits that are often employed. In effect, this imposes a tax on all users of dollars, as each new dollar printed serves to devalue those already in existence.

Not surprisingly, the price of gold rose during the 1970s until 1978, when it broke through $200 per ounce. Americans, who had only become permitted to legally own gold again in 1974 after FDR passed legal action to confiscate gold in 1933, caught gold fever and saw gold ownership as a relief from the inflation of the '70s. Such an irrational mania was bound to end in disaster, and by the end of the decade, gold had peaked at more than 24 times its price under Bretton Woods, valuing the metal around $850 per ounce. Interestingly, because of the increased price, the U.S. had a chance to go back on the gold standard at this time. The value of the gold in storage in the U.S. Treasury became high enough to be able to back the currency in circulation. But no one seemed to notice, and when the value of gold in dollars sank again during the 1980s, the opportunity was missed.

Not everyone agrees that the gold standard is necessary for fiscal discipline, and arguably it should not be, even though to not have it requires voluntary restraint by each successive government, in contrast to the enforced discipline the gold standard does offer. Warren Buffett, one of the world's greatest stock market investors, has said the gold standard is not viable, and his comments show little respect for gold, pointing out that the utility of gold is not high, and that the metal has not been a very good investment over the last century. He feels that gold can act as a check on economic excesses, but can also be a restraint to necessary economic activity. Buffett was named the richest person in the world in 2008 by *Forbes* magazine.

The late '70s were also a time of economic crisis, which further drove the frenzy for gold ownership, creating a demand that fueled the soaring price. President Ronald Reagan came to power, the interest rates rose substantially, and gold dropped to less than half its recent level. The U.S. entered a period of high unemployment, high interest rates, and high inflation.

To some extent, high inflation requires high interest rates, a fact that Paul Vocker, the chairman of the Fed in 1979 realized. Unless the interest rates are high — higher than inflation — then any money invested loses its value. The real rate of return on money invested is the interest rate less the inflation rate. For example, if the inflation rate is 4 percent, and the interest rate is 6 percent, then you would have a 2 percent return on investment. If the rates were the opposite, a 6 percent inflation rate and a 4 percent interest rate, then your return on investment would be -2 percent, meaning that your money is losing its value.

Even so, a high interest rate tends to attract foreign investors into dollar investments, and the dollar strengthened during this period. The strong dollar made the price of gold drop in comparison. The problem with the imbalance in the economy was that the rates made the recession worse, presenting President Reagan with a substantial problem when he entered office.

In an effort to resolve the situation, the Fed increased the currency supply significantly and reduced interest rates, and both actions had the effect of encouraging expenditure. In 1987, the U.S. became the world's greatest debtor nation, increasing the national debt to more than $2 trillion. Realizing the problem of increasing inflation, the Fed raised short-term interest rates, too late, and this was followed by the stock market crash on Monday, October 19, 1987, also known as Black Monday. The Dow lost more than 20 percent on that day, and markets around the world were similarly affected.

At this time, the fear was that the world would fall into a depression, so the Fed increased the currency supply again, taking it even further away from the security of a gold standard because the Fed was supplying more currency than could be backed by gold. All this manipulation of the currency was having dramatic effects on the economy. The real estate boom at the end of the '80s was a result of the increasing currency supply. To control this, the Fed began raising interest rates from 6.5 percent to nearly 10 percent by the beginning of 1989, which over-corrected the situation and caused a property bust.

The savings and loan crisis of 1988, which required a $300 billion bailout, and Operation Desert Storm, at the beginning of 1991, ensured that the United States cranked up the rate of deficit spending, and the national debt rose to nearly $4 trillion. The economy was inexorably beating a path toward further ruin. As described in earlier examples, once the gold standard has been discarded, it is sometimes only a matter of time before the fiat currency (money used in circulation as declared by the government) reveals its worthlessness.

You may be wondering what was happening to the price of gold during this time. It was keeping a low profile, due in part to forward selling by mining companies. *Read a further explanation of this in Chapter Three.* Forward selling means agreeing to a contract with a price long before the sale takes place. From the mining companies' perspective, this agreement hedges their risk that gold would drop further in value, and ensures that it is economical for them to continue mining. For the buyer of the contract, they are assured that they will be able to buy gold at a reasonable price in the future, and not be caught out by a rapid increase in price, which might slow their business of selling gold to the retail consumers. When President Bill Clinton entered office, gold was selling for about $350 per ounce. Thus, any agreements made with mining companies before this time would guarantee that the price they received for gold reflected the higher price that gold was valued at under Bretton Woods.

During the last decade of the twentieth century, the price of gold fluctuated for various reasons. There was a steady demand for the metal, which sustained the price through the mid-'90s, but events in 1998 and 1999 pushed the price back down. In 1998, Russia defaulted on its debts — a matter of some concern to Long-Term Capital Management, a hedge fund that failed as a direct result, losing $4.6 billion in less than four months. This was despite the fact that the Board of Long-Term Capital Management had two Nobel Prize-winning economists. In 1999, the Bank of England decided to sell over half of its gold reserves at auction, in hindsight an absurd tactic guaranteed to lose money for the bank, as the massive influx of gold on the market pushed the price down. The price fell to about $250 per ounce for a short time.

Since that time, gold has been quite steadily increasing in value with less wild fluctuations. The dramatic tales of the Fed manipulations and their impacts serve to show how a fiat currency is seen by some as a precarious experiment that is only a small step away from instability. The answer to this, according to Steve Forbes in an interview published in *The Daily Reckoning* in early 2009, is to base your monetary policy on the price of gold. If it goes up, you are printing too much money, and if it goes down, you are not creating enough credit for the needs of the economy. He agrees with Warren Buffett that the gold standard is not necessary, but argues for a stable value for the dollar using a system as outlined. Though he ran for president in 1996 and 2000, Forbes is not in a position to control the currency excesses, which are destined to increase gold's price.

RECENT HISTORY

Around the turn of the century, technology allowed for the dot-com boom. That was the time when anyone with an idea in the technology field could incorporate a company, take the company public for a huge sum of money, and enjoy easy living on the proceeds. There was a seemingly irrational exuberance for all things high-tech. With the threat of unforeseen disasters from the Y2K bug, the Fed, under Alan Greenspan, was complicit in this boom, pumping a substantial amount of liquidity into the markets. Many investors lost fortunes with the collapse of companies such as WorldCom and Enron.

Having been beaten up by this false boom, the situation only got worse with the disaster of September 11, the destruction of the World Trade Center. History will show how much this was to blame for further devaluation in the U.S. dollar. The amount of currency that has been invented as a result of this attack — for instance, to fund a multi-year war in Iraq and Afghanistan — is considered a factor, by some, that leads the country farther down the path of dollar devaluation, price inflation, and perhaps eventually a currency collapse.

As if this were not enough to destroy the currency, the money supply more than doubled in a decade from 1995 to 2005, fueling the housing bubble. Adjustable rate mortgages, no down payment deals, and much looser qualifying standards all contributed to the boom in housing, soaring prices, and the inevitable collapse. Through all of this, gold has maintained its value, even though the price has fluctuated. In 2009, gold broke the psychological $1,000 barrier, and many pundits said that this released it to climb to much greater heights. *There is more on the technical concepts of support and resistance to price movement in Chapter Eleven.*

In this respect, it is important to differentiate between value and price. In truth, the price means very little, even though it is the factor used to gauge necessity when talking about the trading markets. Gold has an enduring value, regardless of how it is priced at any particular moment in history.

THE FUTURE OUTLOOK

At the time of writing this book, there appears to be a general consensus of opinion that gold is on the way up in terms of price, even as the price experiences slight decreases and increases from day to day. How quickly and how far are matters of debate. There is no such thing as a sure thing; otherwise, everyone who could read would be rich, and then you would wonder where the money would come from. In fact, the price of gold may go down again before continuing its rise, even though you will not find many pundits who will mention this.

As you can see from the history, gold deserves to keep rising in price, and one day the fiat currency may even collapse entirely, making those doomsday prophets who say you should own gold and silver coins for emergency spending correct. But this prophecy is to deny the fact that the government and the Fed will do everything in their power to feign stability in the system, and the collapse may therefore take a long time in coming. In effect, gold is the ultimate buy-and-hold investment.

Regarding the levels to which gold may soar, opinions vary wildly. Some experts are content to use technical analysis, dissecting the charts with such devices as Fibonacci lines to give projections of pivotal prices. *A technical analysis of these projections will be discussed in Chapter Six to see what that can reveal.* Technical analysis by its very nature deals with relatively short-term price movements and is most frequently associated with traders. It is no surprise that these analysts may target $1,200 as the next goal, for instance.

Other analysts would seek to take a longer-term view, placing more emphasis on fundamental factors, such as those discussed above. These are still subject to a great deal of individual interpretation, particularly in the light of the massive company bailouts of 2009, which have involved the creation of phenomenal amounts of money. The calculations are not quite as simple as reviewing the amount of gold in the Treasury and the amount of currency in circulation, and dividing through to establish a price, although that is the only exercise that would restore currency stability. Longer-term valuations have ranged from $2,300 to over $6,000 per ounce from one proclaimed expert.

The reason for such massive variations in estimate is that the path of gold's price is far from predictable for those on the outside, and hard to control for those on the inside. What this means is that most central governments have stores of gold as a reserve, even though there is no official gold standard anymore. It would be naïve to believe that they will not use those stores as they see fit to manipulate the price of gold. We have seen this effect already in 1999 when the Bank of England sold half of its reserves with the result that the price went down to $250 per ounce. Following this, a number of European Central Banks decided to place a cap on sales of gold, and the price shot up to $340 before 1999 was over.

It is also highly possible that there will be another gold rush, such as in the '70s, when everyone realizes it is right to be positioned in gold and the price is driven by demand to heights that cannot be justified in the long-term. It is the nature of trading that the public responds to fads in an excessive way, and the majority of people jump on the train together — too late — to achieve maximum profit. The question is, how do you become positioned in gold to achieve the maximum benefits and avoid false values? The remaining chapters of this book address the different ways this can be done.

Supply and demand

Setting aside for one moment the inexorable path to currency collapse — which mandates that, in the long run, physical things, such as gold, commodities, and real estate, will become immensely more valuable than the printed pieces of paper that we currently use for commerce — there are more reasons why gold, in particular, and other precious metals, may be looked to for prospect of immediate gain.

Most people understand the basics of supply and demand, which is the basis of much economic thinking. The principle is easily explained and worth considering. The economist will demonstrate this with the chart of supply of some goods compared with the price of those goods. When the price that will be paid for the goods increases, then the chart shows that there will be a greater supply. This is intuitive, as more people would make the goods if the price increased, and if the price went lower, fewer people would find it worth their time to make the goods, causing the supply to fall.

The demand chart is at odds with this. If the price of the goods were very low, then there would be a large demand, with everyone thinking that they wanted more of it. At the other end, when the price is really high, hardly anyone wants to buy it, and the quantity demanded will drop. The power of the supply and demand theory comes when you combine the two charts and examine the point where the supply and demand lines cross. This represents the stable position of how much of the product is needed, and how much you can sell it for. The suppliers are happy to supply that number of items at the stated price, and the consumers want to buy that many. Though you would expect some fluctuation over time, the system is self-regulating and will tend toward the line of crossing.

If there is an external influence that affects the supply or demand, then the quantities adjust to seek equilibrium again. If there is a shortage of supply, or an increase in demand, then the price will go up; if there is a glut, or nobody wants it anymore, then the price must come down over time.

Considering the last several decades, there has been a significant drop in supply of gold. Years of falling prices meant that there was not much money put into production and exploration. The production of gold peaked in 2001 but has since experienced a somewhat steady decline. *Learn more about this period in Chapter Three.* The prices rose again, and even though mining became more profitable, it can take as long as seven to ten years to develop new mines and production facilities.

Another factor in increasing production is that most of the easily mined metal has been retrieved over the centuries, so future production will require increasingly more difficult techniques. It is not generally realized how little gold there is in the world. If all the gold ever mined were spread over a football field, then it would only be 5 feet high.

Along with falling supply, there is a strong demand for gold. For instance, India and China are becoming increasingly involved with trading internationally and growing as societies. Their newfound wealth and their booming middle class add to the demand for gold and silver jewelry, and in these countries it is even more prized than in the U.S. Jewelry is the major market for gold and has consumed more than the mine production in the last few years, which leaves nothing for other requirements, such as industrial processes, legal tender coins, central bank purchases, or electronics.

If you add into this equation the number of people who are concerned by the world economic situation and see investing in gold as insurance against the risks in the market, perhaps as you do, then you can see there is a strong force acting to boost the price of gold in the next few years. In fact, in their September 2007 report, the World Gold Council identified that the demand for investment gold overtook the jewelry demand for the first time.

In case you think that all this talk of supply and demand is exaggerated, you can look at the latest numbers on the Internet, at **www.virtualmetals.co.uk**. This Web site, run by the VM Group and Fortis Bank, has open access and allows anyone to look at the data over the years. At the time of writing, the latest report on gold was issued in late 2009. The following figures were included in the report among the world's total physical supply and demand of gold:

Year	2004	2005	2006	2007	2008	2009
Mine supply	2,409	2,477	2,425	2,398	2,356	2,432
Total demand	4,455	4,385	3,992	3,959	3,796	3,933
Shortfall	**2,046**	**1,908**	**1,567**	**1,561**	**1,440**	**1,501**
Gold physical supply and demand (tons) – world market						

You can see that the shortfall was getting better until late 2009, when this chart was last updated before this book's publication, but there is still a big gap between the amount of gold that is being brought into the world through mining and the amount that is being used each year. As of 2009, the shortfall was growing, which could be in response to an increased demand of gold because of its market performance. The shortfall, as calculated by subtracting the mine supply from the total demand, tells the amount of gold that there is not enough supply for worldwide. The Web site gives a lot more information, including breakdowns by region, by country, and a further breakdown of the uses of the gold.

Of course, the shortfall is made up year by year from other sources, such as scrap recycling and sales from central banks, but these are limited resources that provide a stopgap to make up for the lack of production. It is uncertain how quickly that gap will be filled by bringing new mines on the line, but as previously stated, this is a capital-intensive and time-consuming endeavor, so there will not be an immediate respite from the situation. In 2007, South Africa lost its position as the world's largest producer, and in 2008 many mines in South Africa were unable to maintain full production because of problems with the national power supplier. With mines more than 2 miles deep, a lack of power can be extremely hazardous and certainly disruptive. Power is used not only for the normal industrial processes, but for essential services such as cooling and ventilation, as well as transporting men up and down within the mine. Although for safety reasons mines have emergency power backup, this is not intended to be used for normal production of daily schedules.

To get an idea of the scale of the problem, it is probably worth noting that the United States — the world's largest holder of gold reserves — has around 8,000 tons in store. With a shortfall of 1,000 to 2,000 tons each year, it would not take long to go through the reserves. The potential problem that this creates for investors is perhaps the reason for new investment developments, such as digital gold, or may even be a reason for investors to diversify, using different vehicles for their savings. Your investment options, as an investor, will be discussed throughout this book, but first, you should understand where gold comes from and why the world is subject to shortfalls from the reserves to help you decide which investment types are the best for you.

CHAPTER THREE

Where it Comes From

MINING — THE START

When talking about gold mining, many people think of South Africa. For many years it has been a major producer, as 80 percent of the world's gold supply came from South Africa in 1970. What many people do not know is that since the second half of 2007, it has not been the main producer of gold — China has now taken that title. In the last 30 or 40 years, the output from South African mines has shrunk to about a quarter of what it was. South Africa almost exclusively has underground mining, with some mines more than 2 miles deep.

Gold can also be found in open-pit mining and of course can even be panned for in rivers and flowing water. The use of gold for ornamental and sacred items can be traced back to the fifth century BC, and it is thought that this gold must have been in the accessible places. Even so, there is some evidence that suggests Egyptians were mining gold underground as early as 2000 BC.

Even in biblical times it seemed that about 30,000 ounces of gold were mined every year, and the Bible has hundreds of references to gold. The "golden calf," for instance, was created and worshiped by Moses' people while he was receiving the Ten Commandments. Since these times, gold has always been a symbol of power.

Because gold does not deteriorate and has always been regarded as valuable, almost all the gold ever mined is still in existence in a useful or decorative form. Estimates of the amount of gold in the world are difficult to make, but one source puts the amount at 39 million ounces at the beginning of the nineteenth century, 226 million ounces at the beginning of the twentieth century, and an enormous 3 billion ounces by the start of the twenty-first century.

There was a surge in production of gold around the middle of the nineteenth century, when the gold rush took hold in America and Australia. This facilitated most countries adopting the gold standard, which in some cases took the place of silver coins used before. Mining in both the U.S. and Australia is more typically the open-pit type of mine, a process that scrapes away layers of the earth to create a deep pit used for extracting gold. Some of these open-pit mines, however, may subsequently become underground when the mine matures and further reserves are sought.

Mining has always been difficult and is still dangerous, even though the methods of mining have changed appreciably over the years. In particular, with underground mining there is the danger of earthquakes, which can cause rock movements. There are also high temperatures that are experienced as you go deep underground, which without cooling would exceed the daytime temperatures in Arizona, where the average high is around 105 degrees during summer. Then, of course, there is the need to provide clean air for miners to breath, which is unpolluted by carbon dioxide or methane. All these problems can cause significant difficulties given the current depths of mines like the ones in South Africa.

There are also dangers associated with open-pit mining, as explosives are used to extract materials of the earth, though not the same as being deep underground. But in either case, there is a logistical problem because of the sheer amount of ore — the rock that minerals, like gold, are extracted from — that needs to be extracted to retrieve a small amount of gold. In this respect, underground mining is more efficient. Typically a seam of ore will yield about 10 grams of gold per ton, or 1 ounce of gold for every 3 tons. For a typical open-pit mine, 1 ounce of gold may require 60 tons of ore to be milled and treated.

Not that this is the only problem. The quantity of dirt that has to be processed has caused environmental concerns, including campaigns to clean up and control the way gold is extracted. These involve chemical processes, and one of the chemicals involved is cyanide.

One of the calculations that mine owners will continually reassess is the cost of extracting gold in harder-to-reach or less rich veins. When talking about the amount of gold left in a mine, the industry will call the amount readily available at current prices the size of the "reserves." This is not the total amount of gold in the mine, as the gold containing ore does not abruptly finish.

Some gold is more costly to extract because the ore contains a lower percentage of gold or is harder to reach; this gold is called the additional "resources" of the mine. Such gold will not be extracted, at least using present technology, and must wait until the price of gold is such that recovery of it is economic, assuming no cheaper means of retrieving it is invented.

Actual annual gold production was a maximum in 2001 at 2,650 metric tons. It had increased steadily from about 1,000 tons a year in the '50s to around 2,400 in the '90s, a value to which it has dropped back recently. The amount of gold produced is a result of the price that can be achieved within physical limitations of the maximum rate. Extraction will only go ahead to the extent that it is profitable, and mining operations are heavily capitalized with an appreciable time lag between the initial investment and profitable production.

In the case of the falloff in production in this century, the key factor appears to have been the price of gold in the '90s, which was not sufficient to encourage fresh exploration. A further factor was a scandal involving a company called Bre-X Minerals, which falsely claimed a major discovery of gold. When the scam was discovered, venture capitalists were annoyed and turned their attention to the then-profitable technology sector, which meant that almost all exploration ceased between 1997 and 2001.

There are two types of companies in the gold mining field. *Learn more in the section on mining stocks in Chapter Five.* One is the small entrepreneurial exploration company, where their work may be rewarded by a massive find, or they may go bankrupt in the absence of any gold discovery. The larger type of mining firm is more concerned with the physical extraction, and will often buy the small company's discovery rather than speculating with its own exploration.

Operating costs for gold mining have increased significantly in recent years. It is estimated that the average cost of production was approximately $170 per ounce in 2001, and this rose to about $300 per ounce by 2006. There are several factors influencing this rise, including the rise in fuel costs, construction costs, and chemicals for gold separation. With the current level of prices, in 2009, it is obviously worthwhile for mining companies to produce gold at the maximum rate their equipment can handle, but it is easy to see why there may have been reticence at certain times in the past.

REFINING

The process of extracting gold ore from a mine and turning it into gold that can be sold on the market is progressive, especially as gold becomes more refined at each step until it reaches the required level of purity.

First of all, when the ore is transported to the surface, it is crushed to allow chemical treatment. Typically, the crushed ore is treated with a solution of sodium cyanide, which dissolves the metals in the ore, including gold and silver. This solution is pumped through tanks containing carbon granules, which attract and retain the dissolved gold-cyanide compound. The cyanide solution is recirculated to continue the process.

The gold mixture is then dissolved in an alkaline solution and re-deposited onto a cathode by an electrolytic process. After melting in a refinery furnace, which separates the gold and silver from nonmetallic substances, the gold is approximately 90 percent pure and is formed into "doré bars." Despite the processing that has taken place, the gold is far from ready for sale to the jewelry trade or any other dealer, and it must be shipped to a specialist refinery for further processing.

There are many refineries in the world, and it depends on the standard to which the gold is to be prepared which one will be used. The chief benchmark for quality is set out by the London Bullion Market Association (LBMA) on their Web site **www. LBMA.org.uk** and is known as the London Good Delivery gold bar. There are just 57 refineries in the world that are acceptable to the association for production of this, the recognized international standard. However, different countries have different purity and weight requirements, so the gold will be prepared with its final destination in mind.

Typically, in a refinery the gold in the form of the doré bars will be heated in crucibles until it becomes molten, and then treated with chlorine gas. The chlorine does not react with gold, but bonds with impurities, base metals, and even silver to form chlorides. These chlorides then float to the surface of the molten gold, where they are removed as slag or escape as gases. The process takes a couple of hours and will produce gold that is at least 99.5 percent pure, with silver as the next largest constituent. This gold is sufficiently pure to be made into London Good Delivery gold bars.

Some markets require gold of much greater purity, sometimes as much as 99.99 percent pure, commonly known as "four nines gold," and there are electrolytic processes to achieve this.

The London Good Delivery gold bar is the one with which you will be most familiar, as replicas of this are featured in most good bank robbery films. When made of gold, the bar weighs roughly 400 troy ounces (1 troy ounce is equivalent to 1.097 ounces), and is about 10 inches long, 2 ¾ inches wide, and 1 ¾ inches thick. Each bar has a serial number, the refiner's stamp, year of manufacture, and purity, but typically will not have the weight marked on it by the refiner. The LBMA strongly recommends that each bar is weighed in London by an approved weigher to determine the exact content.

CASE STUDY: GARY FRENKEL

Gary Frenkel - President Midwest Refineries, LLC
4471 Forest Ave.
Waterford, MI 48328
1-800-356-2955
www.midwestrefineries.com

Midwest Refineries, LLC set its standard in the precious metals refinery industry when the family business opened in 1939. The third generation of family-ownership under company president Gary Frenkel continues to put that standard into daily business practice.

Midwest Refineries serves a gamut of industries in addition to the general public and prides itself on no order being too small or too large. The company offers a myriad of services for owners of precious metals. Midwest Refineries buys, smelts, refines, essays, and brokers precious metals, including gold, silver, rhodium, palladium, and platinum.

The company's Web site at **www.midwestrefineries.com** provides a full description of the services offered, as well as educational information about assaying and other aspects of precious metals.

Frenkel recommends that individuals who want to sell their gold or other precious metal to a refinery make sure they first know that they could be charged for the following services:

1. Refining fees
2. Assaying fees
3. Treatment charges
4. Brokerage fees
5. Inbound troy-ounce weight fees
6. Handling fees

Understand that companies that may claim to pay virtually 100 percent of the price of pure gold or other expensive metal, like platinum, could very well charge these fees, which would distort the percentage of the price they are actually charging.

What else you need to know before you send your gold and other precious metal items to a refinery:

1. Always include all your contact information when sending gold items. The information should include your name, address, daytime phone number, and e-mail address.

2. It is not necessary to list every item you are sending, but do state the type of material you are sending if you know it, such as 10K or 14K gold, sterling silver, or platinum wire, as well as the weight of the material.

3. Always use a sturdy container or box that will withstand the shipping process, and make sure you properly seal the container with strong tape.

4. Insure your metals when you ship them.

5. Indicate your settlement choice. Do you want to be paid by check, bank wire, precious metals bars, coins, rounds, or a combination of any of these?

Because gold itself does not depreciate, the precious metal is able to maintain its intrinsic value. When that is added to gold's market value, many start to take notice of its performance, therefore shaping the metal into a variety of forms after it is extracted and refined. These physical forms of gold are just some of the ways you can choose to invest.

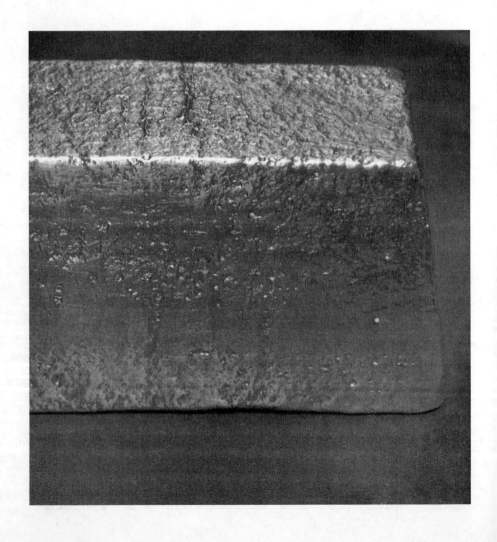

CHAPTER FOUR

The Shape of Gold

A fter production and refining, gold is put to many different uses, and you have many choices of which form to buy, even if you are investing in gold as a substance, as opposed to as a component used in the manufacture of something else.

BULK GOLD

The most obvious form in which to own a significant amount of gold is as gold bullion — meaning as bars or ingots, which are thicker gold bars that are cast rather than stamped. These have the advantage of being relatively compact and easy to store, although you may want to keep them in a safety deposit box rather than around the house. Your choice of location may be influenced by your view of the future — if you believe in the forthcoming crash of society from the collapse of fiat currency and are of the doomsday persuasion, then nothing would stop you from keeping your gold in a safe in your house.

When you buy gold bullion, make sure that the price you pay is close to the quoted or "spot" price of gold in the market. Unlike other forms of physical gold, bullion should not be priced at much of a premium over the price of the metal, which you can look up in the newspaper or online. The premium covers the costs for the seller, and on small orders it will be higher. It is a good idea to buy only from reputable dealers, and you may wish to avoid dealings with private parties, such as the ones advertised on eBay.

Before you buy physical gold, you should do some research to find reputable dealers who have gold at the price you want to pay. The Internet is an easy method to find and investigate such dealers, but as always, with the World Wide Web you need to ensure you have independent corroboration of any published data, as it is not unknown for sellers to fabricate letters of recommendation or good reputations where none should exist. You should look for dealers who have been in business at least five years and who have independently verifiable backgrounds.

When you have found two or three dealers you are interested in, ask each of them to quote for the amount of gold that you want to buy. If you do not find the price you want, then you can try negotiating with the dealer, but be aware that dealers deal in large quantities of gold and are unlikely to discount their price to the small buyer. Depending on the market conditions, you may find that the dealer does not have much time for you, and that you have to fight for their attention. This is especially true if the market conditions are constantly changing, forcing the dealer to have to adapt and re-adapt to the state of the market. Therefore, you should take the time necessary to do the research and find the deal that you want.

Usually when you buy gold bars, you do not have to pay too much more than the value of the weight of gold to purchase them, but if you are looking to buy in bulk, this may not be the most convenient form. For instance, if you buy supplies from a grocery store or a farmer, you would find it very difficult to buy them with a gold bar, whereas a gold or silver coin might be of value in this situation. You need to be clear on your feelings about the future, and also plan for the worst that you expect.

Coinage

Though gold and silver coins were regularly used in earlier times, going back thousands of years, because of the extreme value of the metals, they are not now in common circulation. If you want to buy coinage, you will need to find a dealer, and the same warnings as given above for dealers in ingots apply here. There are many advertisements in the press and in direct mail, and while some of these may be worthwhile, you should take care to shop around and find the best deal for your requirements.

Coin dealers have specialized knowledge, and there are many detailed factors taken into account when valuing a coin. The best examples of coinage are covered by the term "numismatics," and you can also buy semi-numismatic coins, which are not as highly prized but are available at a lower premium over the metal value.

Numismatics

The term numismatics covers the finest examples of coins, or coins that are in supreme condition. These are considered eminently collectible, and in terms of the weight of gold content, they are expensive. However, they are recognized as a good investment in the long-term. Numismatic coins are not for every investor, and you will need to undertake detailed research to be sure that the product you are buying is a suitable and worthwhile investment in your circumstances. The advantage of coins over bullion is obvious because their liquidity is good, which means they can be turned into cash fairly easily. The disadvantage is that you pay a premium for them, so unless the price of gold rises substantially, you may find it is some time before you can get your investment back when you sell.

The wonderful thing about numismatic coins is that you own the finest examples of great artwork, which you can appreciate and admire. Many of the coins are extremely decorative and, apart from their great value and the associated security risk, would be suitable to show off in a display case. If you wish to invest in these, you will need to learn which coins are the most sought-after. You should investigate the market to ensure that there is a reasonable amount of trading in the coins you are interested in so that you can expect to be able to sell fairly readily if you need to. The coinage will always be worth the weight of gold, but the best coins will demand a high premium over this, often unrelated to the actual weight of gold.

If you are serious about collecting coins, you will need to become familiar with the rating system, known as the Sheldon Scale. This will allow you to better understand exactly what you are buying and what you should look for. In general, you will find that most rare numismatic coins should be in the higher ratings, such as MS-66 to 70.

The grading system was the subject of some contention particularly in the 1980s, when it was seen to be somewhat subjective because what one grader considered to be a top-quality coin may not be as close to perfection to another grader. Prior to the 1950s, there was no precise grading system, but coins were known by descriptions such as Good, Fine, Uncirculated, and so on. The Sheldon Scale, invented by William Sheldon in 1948, has become an industry standard that enables comparatively easy evaluation and comparison between different coins. The scale has a numeric system, which goes from 1 to 70, and the numbers are used with initials, which stand for a description. For instance, the MS referred to above stands for Mint State, meaning that there are no flaws.

Although as an investor you will be principally concerned with the better collectible grades of coins (ranging from MS-60 to FDC in the following table), it is interesting to see the extreme range of conditions that are described in this comprehensive scale.

Sheldon grade (From lowest to highest)	What it stands for	Description of coin
P-1	Poor	The worst a coin can be — most of it is worn smooth or badly damage. Only some of the type can barely be made out.
FR-2	Fair	This is not much better than Poor, but the type of coin and date can be made out.
G-3	About Good	This coin is very heavily worn — parts of the design may be smooth, but it is generally discernible. *Some grading scales do not use P-1 and FR-2 and instead use this as the lowest grade.*

G-4	Good	This grade is not really good, but a little better than the worst. The coin is heavily worn, but you can make out most of the features.
G-6	Good-Plus (slightly better than G-4)	The major features of this coin are clear, even though there is heavy wear.
VG-8	Very Good	The coin is still significantly worn but generally readable with clear features.
F-12	Fine	This range has moderate, even wear, and all of the legends are readable.
VF-20, VF-30	Very Fine	These grades have light to medium wear. All of the features on this coin are sharp.
EF-40 (also called XF-40)	Extremely Fine	This grade of coin only shows light wear, with all of the features clear. This is the grade of coin you would want to have if you were a coin collector.
AU-50	About Uncirculated (the lowest level)	These coins are very good-looking, as if they had not been in general circulation. They still show small traces of wear, meaning that they could have been used at some point. They also have some luster.
AU-55	Good About Uncirculated	This grade has less than a trace of wear and has the majority of its luster left (at least half).
AU-58	Choice About Circulated	These coins have hardly any traces of wear marks, and nearly the total mint luster remains. This is nearly the grade an investor would look for.
MS-60	Mint State (spans from 60-70)	This is the quality of coin that should be looked at by a true investor. They are mint coins, sometimes also called uncirculated or UNC. This grade may be without luster and may be marked, making it look far worse than the AU-58, but they are graded as MS because they have not been circulated at all.
MS-70	Mint State (highest)	This is a coin with full luster and is sometimes incorrectly called a Proof coin.

PR-60, PR-70	Proof	This grade actually refers to the method of manufacture of the coins — it was originally intended that proof coins were stamped to prove the design was correct, and not for circulation. Thus, proof coins are the sharpest in detail and have brilliant mirror surfaces.
FDC	Fleur de Coin	This is a proof coin that is absolutely perfect in every way.

You may be interested that as of October 2009, the U.S. Mint has declared that because of unprecedented demand, it is unable to provide proof and uncirculated versions of the 1-ounce American Eagle coins. Production has been ceased so that bullion coins can be produced from the available 22-carat gold blanks. The Mint is said to be working diligently with suppliers of the blanks so that production can recommence in 2010. This suggests that many people are turning to gold investment as a hedge against the financial system.

The Mint is compelled to produce the bullion coins by Public Law 99-185. The law directs the agency to produce these coins in quantities sufficient to meet the demand of the public, and shortage of supplies means production of the specialized versions of the coins, the proof and uncirculated, has had to be abandoned for at least the rest of 2009.

Numismatic coins are the rarest and most collectible investment quality coins that you will find. They are actually legal tender coins that were minted a long time ago, and the last ones issued by the U.S. mint were made in the 1930s. Because of this, they are in short supply, and the prices tend to have little relation to the price of gold per ounce. The premiums that you pay for the coins are also far higher than with lesser coins. Most of them are graded from MS-66 to MS-70, and they include everything up to museum-quality coins.

Investing in rare coins, while it is a part of investing in gold and included in this book, is a subject that would require much more detailed knowledge than what can be included in the scope of this book. You must realize that investing in rare coins is not a trading opportunity, but something that the long-term investor will look at. Because of the premium you pay, it may take several years after you buy them before you could even sell them for a profit. This means that typically you will not want them to be a significant part of your portfolio. When you buy rare coins, there is a significant markup, often up to 15 percent. Nonetheless, you should buy from a reputable dealer, even though they may quote a higher price than some others, as then you have some assurance that the coins are what they are claimed to be in terms of the grading.

You may have noticed that there are many advertisements for this type of investment, and you need to take care that you do not get scammed when buying rare coins. Be particularly careful if you find one dealer is significantly cheaper, as with a well-defined market and legitimate products, you should find that the price is fairly consistent from one seller to another. While the coins may be rare in comparison to others, you can research and find out how many were minted for any particular year, and so get some idea of the rarity value and premium you should pay.

The most important part of valuing a coin is the grading. While you can perform your own rough estimate of the grade from the information given above with the Sheldon Scale, you should look for a professional grading on any coins that you buy, and always buy the best grade that you can afford. There are several professional grading services, and arguably the best respected are the Professional Coin Grading Service and the Numismatic Guaranty Corporation. These will ensure accurate and authentic grading, which will be important when you come to sell.

When a coin is graded, it is examined by numismatic experts and compared to a number of strict guidelines. The grade of the coin is determined and certified, and the individual coin is sealed in a tamper-evident plastic sleeve, which contains information on the company performing the grading and the grade determined. Remember, for investment you will be looking for a grade between 60 and 70, and preferably higher than 65.

It is really important that you purchase a coin that is professionally certified, particularly if you are not experienced in coin collecting. It would be unusual to find a coin that has not been graded, and for you to manage to purchase it for much less than its real value. You are far more likely to lose money if you take a chance on the grade. When a coin is certified, both you and the dealer know exactly what you are dealing with, and price negotiations will be straightforward and fair to both parties. The premium that you pay over the value of the gold in the coin is based on the grade, the rarity, and the popularity of the coin. The premium is considered an additional price you pay to receive the coin, and depends on where the coin was manufactured and distributed, as well as the administration costs that were associated with its production. With the better examples of coins, the actual weight of gold has less relevance to the value than do the other factors.

Though your personal preference may play a role in your coin-purchasing decisions, it is important from an investment point of view that you buy coins that are appealing to investors and collectors. There are some extremely rare coins that are not too expensive because no one cares to purchase or collect them, yet some pennies and nickels are popular with collectors and sell for a substantial premium, as they are in high demand. Coins in poor condition will always be worth close to the metal value, but for an active market when you come to sell, you need to invest in the highest quality coin you can afford, as these are much more likely to be sought after.

Some of the more popular coins that you will see for sale that are still reasonable enough for the average investor to buy are:

- $20 Saint-Gaudens double eagle
- $10 Indian head
- $5 Indian head
- $20 Liberty
- $1 Liberty head

Coins are often known or named by the designs, but are also sometimes called after their designers, as with the Saint-Gaudens, which was named after Augustus Saint-Gaudens.

Semi-numismatic

Semi-numismatic coins are sometimes overlooked, but they are worth investigating. They are not as expensive or as rare as numismatic coins, and frequently will be graded up to MS-65. The premium for these coins is significantly less than for numismatics, and their pricing bears a much closer relationship to the gold content.

The lowest price for these coins is based on the bullion value and can go up from there, depending on the quality and the collectability. For many people they are a better bet than numismatic coins, as you will not be paying a large premium, and these are a safe and convenient way of holding the metal.

An interesting fact is that you will not be involved with reporting requirements and the IRS when you deal in these or numismatic coins. There is an exemption for rare coins, which they set at a level of a premium of 15 percent or greater. Coin dealers do not have to report to the IRS when you buy and sell to them. According to U.S. Rare Coin Investments, **www.usrarecoininvestments. com**, under U.S. tax laws, the individual sales of rare coins, or numismatic coins, do not need to be reported to the IRS by the person who buys them. The sellers of these coins, however, are required to report such transactions, in terms of gains or losses, on their individual tax returns.

This may also be relevant if the government returns to a policy of confiscation. This eventuality is unlikely, but as explained in the history, there is a precedent for gold confiscation, so it cannot be ruled out. Since the mid-'70s, the general public has been allowed to own gold bullion, but it is this that would be confiscated in the event of government action. If history is any guide, it would not apply to numismatic and semi-numismatic gold coins, and an exemption would be made for "gold coins having a recognized special value to collectors of rare and unusual coins." In fact, only 5 percent of all the gold in the U.S. is in the form of collectible coins;

therefore, it may not be worth the government's time to bother confiscating these.

The fact that these deals are not reportable also addresses a matter of some concern to many people. It is the question of personal privacy, and how much the government may know about your financial affairs. Many people would prefer to stay away from the regulations and laws that require the reporting of many financial transactions, and semi-numismatic coins would provide that privacy because you are not legally required to report those transactions.

Bullion

There is a third class of coin that is much more readily obtainable, and that is invested in frequently. This type of coin is called a bullion coin. This is an easy way to purchase small quantities of gold or other precious metal without paying too much of a premium over the material value. You are probably familiar with the term bullion referring to gold or silver in bulk ingot form. It is actually derived from the French word "bouillon," which is nowadays more particularly used when cooking, which means boiling and is associated with melting the gold. Bullion coins are contemporary and are freely minted for sale as investments.

The disadvantage with bullion coins, at least for some people, is that when you sell them to a coin dealer, the dealer is required to report the deal to the IRS on Form 1099. This is because you are not paying a great premium over the value of the metal, and therefore you are trading the metal as far as the government is concerned. There are many examples of recent coin issues that fall into this category. This includes the commemorative coins that are often offered to the public to celebrate a celebrity or a famous event. Although they are labeled as collectibles in order to allow the seller to charge a high price, in reality they should be regarded more from the point of view of bullion coins and valued close to the metal content, which is the intrinsic value of the gold before it enters any type of circulation, with few exceptions.

Bullion coins include such well-known items as the South African Krugerrand. Introduced in the 1960s, this is freely traded and has a low premium compared to other bullion coins. The South African Mint sells them for usually about a 3 to 5 percent premium, subject to minimum quantities and shipping costs, but will only deal with banks and dealers. A popular alternative is the British gold sovereign, which has only a 1 or 2 percent higher premium than the Krugerrand when bought in quantity. This may also be easier to sell.

Despite the reporting situation, for many people bullion coins may be the best way to have some gold that is easily tradable and that can be kept on hand for an emergency. The great advantage is that you do not need to worry about specialist knowledge in knowing whether you have paid the right price, as you do with numismatic coins. Bullion coins track closely to the metal price and represent trading the metal. The premium may range from 2 percent to 10 percent. It is important to remember that regardless of the type of coins you invest in, you will face the same problem of avoiding theft. If you intend to keep the coins at home, as you probably should if you are investing in them in case of an emergency, you should look into security arrangements, and whether a floor or wall safe would be more suitable for your house. These types of security arrangements are discussed later in this chapter.

Jewelry

No book on investing in gold would be complete without mentioning jewelry, as the metal has been recognized for thousands of years as a fundamental component of personal decoration. In fact, the jewelry industry has been the major consumer of newly mined gold for the last couple of decades. As such, jewelry is the most significant demand driver there is for gold, and that demand is mainly in India and China. In India, gold-giving holidays are a long-standing tradition, and people are much more likely to wear their wealth. The markups on jewelry are also significantly lower than in the U.S.

Jewelry is not a particularly efficient way to invest in precious metals. Most jewelry is worth significantly less than the retail price you pay for it, in terms of the metal content, and it is difficult to sell if you want to get some cash. Only experts can identify the quality and value of an item of jewelry.

Gold is a relatively soft metal and is subject to damage in its purest form. That is why you will find different purity standards being used for the gold in jewelry. The most common measure you will find is the carat system. This will tell you how much gold there is in an item, although it does not address what other metal has been mixed with the gold.

The purest gold that you will find in jewelry is called 24 carat, and that is over 99 percent pure. Frequently, you will find 18 carat is used, and this is much more durable, particularly for jewelry that will be worn often. However, this is only 75 percent gold. Another measure you will see is 9 carat, and this is 37.5 percent gold — just half as much. You may be surprised to find how little the gold in your jewelry is worth compared with the cost of buying it. You can easily figure this by multiplying the weight of the jewelry times 0.375 (if it is 9 carats and 37.5 percent pure), and multiplying this by the current price of gold given in the newspaper or on the Internet. For example, if you have a gold necklace that is 9 carats, and you were determining your necklace's value based on the November 2009 price of gold at $1,110 per ounce, you would do the following:

$$.0375 \text{ X } (\$1,110/\text{ounce}) = \$41.625$$

The value, as you can tell, most likely will not represent the price you paid for the necklace. This is why many people are disappointed when they respond to advertisements offering to buy gold.

Physical storage

As you will discover throughout this book, there are other ways in which you can invest in gold or gold-related financial instruments that do not involve the actual metal. All the forms discussed so far involve taking possession of the physical item. Thus, it is worth considering how this is best achieved, and the advantages and disadvantages of the various ways.

When you purchase physical gold and other precious metals, you also have the responsibility for keeping those assets safe. The ultimate goal is to store them safely in a manner that prevents them from being stolen or damaged by accident. If you decide to purchase physical gold or precious metals, you need to determine in advance what you will do with these tangible assets.

Bank storage

Although there are some disadvantages, probably one of the safest and most practical methods of storing your gold is to rent a safety deposit box at your bank. This will almost certainly be safer than storing the gold at home, even though thieves know to look in a bank for items of value, and you may manage to keep your possession of gold at home a secret. Typically, a bank robbery will involve stealing cash and other bulk items of value, and the thieves may not have time to examine every safety deposit box, particularly as many may contain documents for a person's security, which are of no immediate value to the thief.

The downside of storing your gold in a bank, however, is that there are times when is the bank will be closed and you will not be able to retrieve your items. This may mean that you are unable to get your hands on your gold and precious metals when you most need them, for example, at times of civil unrest. To resolve this, some investors will keep the bulk of their physical investment in a safety deposit box, while having a supply on hand at home or in another location for emergencies. It can provide some peace of mind to know that you will have immediate access to some of your gold and precious metals investments.

Another possible disadvantage depends on your level of concern that there may be cause for government confiscation in the future. If the government makes it illegal for individuals to hold gold, as they did in the '30s, then one of the first places government officials are likely to look for gold is in a bank safety deposit boxes. With the number of bank collapses that are being experienced at the moment, you may also be concerned about having continued access. The sort of situation where you may need quick access to your gold is likely the same sort of situation that would cause banks to collapse.

Safe storage

Many investors like to keep their gold and precious metals closer to hand, so they will store them at home in a personal safe. If you decide to follow this course of action, there are some issues that you need to bear in mind. The first one is the type of safe. No matter how good the safe, it is even more secure if the home invader does not know if you have one and where it is located, so it should not be obvious to a casual intruder.

You can choose to use a floor safe, wall safe, or freestanding safe. If using a wall safe, you may want to include some substantial construction around it to avoid its being ripped out and taken away. A floor safe is more secure from this point of view, as it can be surrounded by the concrete slab, which provides no easy access to the other side of it, which you have with the wall safe. A freestanding safe would seem to be less secure, as its position is obvious. If you have ever tried to move one, you will know they are not easy to shift, even if they are not fixed down. But, you lose the element of disguise by taking this admittedly easier route of using a freestanding safe.

Before you make your final decision on what type of safe to use, you should check with your insurance company and also consider consulting with a bonded safe company for their recommendations. It is quite possible that your homeowners' insurance will not cover the contents of the safe, and you should check specifically whether they can include gold in their coverage.

Some investors consider that storing gold in their house is risky, but want to have it readily accessible without having to go somewhere, like to a bank, and are prepared to store it in another way. These people will sometimes dig a hole in their backyard and deposit their valuables in the hole in a corrosion-proof container. This has the advantage that the thief will not know where to look, although without even the security of a building, you may think that the gold would be vulnerable. It is fairly certain that anything stored this way would not be covered by insurance. You may just want to be sure you have a system for remembering, or marking, the spot where you buried your container.

If confiscation is threatened, this is a method that is adopted by many investors. One disadvantage is that if you die or become incapacitated, the gold may be lost to your heirs unless you leave detailed instructions. The problem then becomes what to do with the instructions so that, to your detriment, they are not found by a miscreant. As an alternative, you can tell a trusted family member of your plan, but there are certainly difficulties to be faced if you choose the burial method for your gold.

Another alternative is a storage program, which many companies will offer. The company that sells you your gold may provide this facility. This appears very convenient because when you sell your investment you will not have to submit the metals for an assay, as they never been out of the possession of the seller. It does not take much imagination to come up with the disadvantages to this method, and more than one company has operated a scam that cheated investors of their money.

If you want to store your metals with the seller, you should take care to find out that the seller is a well-established firm, properly insured and regulated, and preferably with a trust fund and independent trustee for your protection. Even then, you need to check whether the gold you have bought is allocated or unallocated. It is allocated, effectively it has your name on it, and if you sell it in 20 years, it will still be the same piece of gold that you bought. If it is unallocated, it is considered to be a part of the pool of gold that the company holds. This is sometimes called a "fungible" account. For obvious reasons, most investors prefer a "non-fungible" account. Even then, if a major crisis hits, you may be unable to access your store of gold.

CASE STUDY: DAVID W. YOUNG

Wexford Capital Management President
113 Brenton Court
Stephens City, VA 22655
1-877-855-9760
www.wexfordcoin.com

David W. Young is the president of Wexford Capital Management (WCM), which is a Virginia-based company that has served tangible asset investors for over two decades. The company's primary Web site, at **www.wexfordcoin.com**, provides investors with a variety of pertinent information about precious metals investment in addition to details about the services the company offers.

Young maintains an additional Web site, at **www.goldsilverbullion.com**, where he provides specific market commentary for gold and silver investors through sections such as "Bullion Market Insights" and "Physical Versus Paper." A registered investment advisor for 20 years, he professionally prefers the global liquidity and low premiums on purely bullion coins and bars versus the lower liquidity of U.S. rare coins.

"At Wexford Capital, there's currently a $10,000 invoice minimum for bullion coins and bars," Young said. WCM also provides a full, currently priced list of the products that are recommended for purchase. There is a list of qualified bullion coins and bars that are allowed for individual retirement arrangement (IRA) inclusion, and premiums over the spot price of the underlying precious metal are generally less than 15 percent.

At the end of the day, Young said the best way for investors to protect themselves financially is investment in tangible assets in physical form, only due to the uncertainties that exist on many intermediaries that issue financial security certificates. Rare coins, as well as pure bullion coins and bars, are certainly a solid form for investment, especially in economic times that, at the very least, could be characterized as uncertain. Now that financial and paper assets have shown their vulnerability, investors would be wise to trust only that which they can confirm with their own eyes. For many investors, that will boil down to gold, silver, and platinum in the form of coins and bars.

The U.S. rare coin market is also greatly benefiting from the major bull markets the U.S. is experiencing in the primary precious metals: gold and silver. Investing in rare U.S. coins has long been a very successful pursuit. The appeal of these rare coins as an asset class is enhanced by the finite supply of the coins themselves and a steadily increasing demand for them in the U.S. The emergence of third-party grading services for coin condition has, in recent years, added a readily recognizable standard of expert analysis that takes guesswork or substandard opinion out of the equation for investors who buy rare coins, especially the pre-1933 coins that comprise a significant part of Wexford Capital Management's tangible asset program.

Investors in precious metals who consider inclusion of pre-1933 in their portfolios should seek a trustworthy and credentialed dealer, especially one with enhanced purchasing power who has recognized grading agency status and can both quickly and competently locate specific coins that are sought. At Wexford Capital, there is a $3,500 to $5,000 range minimum for coin purchases, which can be initiated through a collectors' services "wish list," or via WCM recommendations, like the $20 Liberty gold dollars of the Reconstruction Era and the rare incuse minted design of the $2.50 Indian Head series.

There is a likelihood that at some point, rare coins will be permitted for allocation in IRAs, at which time the appeal of pre-1933 U.S. coins should be even further enhanced. This would especially be true during a prolonged super-bear market in stocks and bonds — a reality that may force Congress to act.

Until then, the bullion option is a current, very popular option for investors who seek to have precious metals allocated for IRAs. Dealers can prove very instrumental in this process as well because they can use their purchasing power to buy bullion coins like the gold, silver, and platinum American Eagles that are accepted for custodial processing by depositories authorized to handle IRA metals. WCM has personally used Sterling-Trust and FideliTrade/DDSC for precious metals IRAs since 1997.

DIGITAL GOLD

Although by its nature digital gold cannot be physical gold that you can touch, it is included in this section because it is directly based on physical gold and derives its value from the metal. A very recent idea, it nonetheless has traditional roots that are shrouded in early civilization.

The idea of digital gold, though not a new concept, was given new life in January 2007 by Benn Steil, a director of International Economics at the Council on Foreign Relations in an article that appeared in the *Financial Times*. He argued that the dollar is out of date, and that there should be regional currency developing into a world currency. Digital gold, held by private banks, is a step away from the current dependency on fiat currencies and is an international and sustainable means of making payments. He acknowledged that some private banks already existed that allowed global digital gold payments, and thought that these should be utilized more.

The idea is that the private bank will hold physical gold in its vaults that is worth 100 percent of the clients' funds invested. Transactions can then take place electronically with the assurance that the currency used is fully backed by the value of the gold. In other words, it represents a return to a gold standard for currency, with the added feature that it can be used internationally, as transactions take place with fractional gold amounts rather than a nominal country based currency unit, such as the dollar or euro. You should note that this is intrinsically a more secure method of dealing with your money than using your local bank, because of the traditional banking system that only requires a portion of your investment to be held by a bank — the capitalization. *See this further outlined in Chapter Two.* Set against this, however, is the lack of FDIC insurance and of government regulation for these companies, which at least covers your local bank.

Digital gold, however, appears to have the possibility of being one way that the impending collapse in fiat currencies can be avoided, at least for those who embrace this system. It represents a rejection of each individual government's power to generate currency at a whim, and if it takes off, it has the potential to end inflation, at least for transactions in digital gold. As such, it is looking more and more like a sensible solution to what many people see coming: the destruction of the dollar's value by hyperinflation.

Before you fully embrace this concept and transfer all your money to digital gold, remember that it has many of the features that you have been warned against in the earlier parts of this chapter. For instance, with digital gold, you do not at any time hold a piece of gold, but simply have gold that is apparently owned by the bank allocated to you. If the bank were to fail, your claim would be against the bank, and you would have no direct claim on the metal. Therefore, for those who like to have a stash of gold in their possession for security purposes, this option may not be the best way to go. With digital gold, you also rely on the bank to back their operations in full with physical gold without a ready method of testing the value held. As a point of further concern, many of the companies that are becoming involved with and offering digital gold are domiciled, or registered, off-shore outside the U.S.

With all these caveats, it should be noted that digital gold is, thus far, running smoothly and responsibly, so it is up to you to decide whether and when you will consider this investment. In truth, digital gold does not promote itself as an investment, as there is no direct return. But it can be considered an investment in the same way as physical gold because as the value increases, so does digital gold. Therefore, your return on your investment comes into play as the value increases, even though you do not physically own the gold. Digital gold is sometimes referred to as digital gold currency, or DGC, and there is a *DGC Magazine*, which you can find at **http://issuu.com/dgcmagazine/docs**.

As your holding in the bank is measured in terms of gold, there is no problem with currency exchange rates. You are free to ex-change your gold back into the currency of many different coun-tries at the prevailing gold price, less a small commission. Often you can make an arrangement between the Internet-based digi-tal gold bank and your personal bank to allow easy exchange of funds between the two. But because digital gold is generally regarded as a private currency, it can only be exchanged using the following methods:

- Bank wire
- Check
- Direct deposit
- Money order

There are some costs associated with DGC. As mentioned above, there will be a transaction cost when you sell the gold and receive currency, and this typically may be 2 percent of the spot price. There could be other fees if you require a currency in which the bank does not normally deal. Initially, when you buy the gold, you may expect a fee, most probably taken as a spread from the spot price. As you are buying physical gold, you can expect to be charged a monthly storage fee, a fixed charge, or a percentage of the value. If you decide to try digital gold, make sure that you have checked what fees will be applicable to your situation, as the same fees that apply to physical gold may not apply with your bank or broker for digital gold.

There are several large companies in this field, with names like e-gold®, Goldmoney®, BullionVault, and Pecunix. They do have some differences in how they operate, which will be mentioned later in this chapter. For now, you should note that DGC banks do not have any system of support for the consumer if the purchase does not work out correctly. Unlike credit card companies, you cannot dispute a payment. All payments are made instantly. This has the advantage that you know when you receive DGC that you have been paid beyond a doubt — but of course, the disadvantage is when you are paying someone and do not receive satisfaction, you must recourse to legal proceedings if available. It is important to note that some digital gold companies have a notice of risk, stating that you, the person trading or investing in digital gold, assume the responsibility for the investment and other price fluctuations that are beyond the companies' control.

Some of the digital companies do not just use gold as the reserve; several have also ventured into using silver. If the idea of digital gold really becomes popular, there would not be sufficient gold available to meet the demand, as more people would be investing in the digital metal than there is actual gold to represent the investments. Thus, this would present a situation where the Internet DGC bank must look for other precious commodities, such as platinum or silver, in order to fully back the investments made.

One of the original companies set up to provide this digital service, e-gold, is a company run by Gold and Silver Reserve, Inc. It was started in the U.S. by Dr. Douglas Jackson, but subsequently moved to Nevis in the West Indies — one of the most well-known tax havens, despite having an operational center in Florida. It was founded in 1996, but transactions have grown significantly in recent years. The gold is held by an associated trust in allocated storage and amounts to 67,000 ounces at the time of writing. In addition, e-gold holds more than 85,000 ounces of silver, 400 ounces of platinum, and nearly 400 ounces of palladium. These figures are regularly updated on the company's Web site **www.e-gold.com**.

Because of the way they operate, e-gold has no currency and no exchange services. It was conceived as an Internet payment system that could be used worldwide without any financial intermediaries. To make a deposit or buy e-gold, you must use an independent exchange service, which will take your payment in currency and convert it to gold on deposit. They proudly boast on the Web site that "e-gold is the only currency in the world free of financial risk," on the basis that the holdings are entirely backed by a physical commodity. As the Web site also points out, though, there are still currency exchange rate risks. Even when dealing entirely in dollars, your e-gold account will fluctuate daily to allow for gold price fluctuations.

In 2007, the proprietors were indicted by the U.S. Department of Justice on money-laundering questions. In 2008, three directors entered a plea of guilty to some of the charges, and the company was fined. The judge in the case gave lenient sentences because he felt that they did not intend to engage in illegal activity. Subsequently, e-gold has been pursuing licensing as a money-transmitting business where it is deemed required in the states, which is a license for a business to engage in issuing payment instruments. This has had some effect on their operation, and the amount of gold in storage has reduced significantly from previous years, presumably as clients redeemed their accounts in reaction to the news. As of late 2009, they are not accepting any new accounts.

GoldMoney was founded by James Turk in 2001 and is based in Jersey, one of the British Channel Islands frequently used for offshore accounts and tax avoidance. Its Web site is at **www.goldmoney.com**. Part of the application process is to verify your identity, which can be done through Equifax for U.S. and UK residents. The company has a different approach to digital gold, with less emphasis on using their services for transactions and more emphasis toward a convenient method of buying gold and silver.

Unlike digital gold, you can wire funds directly to them, then choose to buy gold or silver for the long-term.

The fees are reasonable, and Turk has a good reputation, as it was previously a merchant banker. The company claims that it had over $759 million worth of gold, silver, and currencies at the end of September 2009. The monthly storage fees they charge are modest, sometimes around 1 percent of the amount of gold that is being stored, and flat rates represent exceptionally good value for larger gold holdings.

The company has also affiliated with Entrust Group to form a way that gold and silver investments can be included in an individual retirement arrangement (IRA), with the associated tax advantages. For UK residents, they have worked a similar deal with Berkeley Burke to include gold in a self-invested personal pension (SIPP).

For UK and European investors, GoldMoney has the added advantage that it is Jersey-based. This represents nearly home territory to the British, who are much more likely to accept this as safe and stable than an island in the middle of the Atlantic Ocean. A further advantage for Europeans is that they can use GoldMoney to invest legally in silver bullion without paying value-added tax (VAT). GoldMoney has a facility to hold an account in local currencies, but it is likely that the fees involved would make any trading not very profitable.

BullionVault was founded by Paul Tustain and is based in the UK. From its Web site, **www.bullionvault.com**, you will notice an interesting feature, which is that the gold is stored in New

York, London, and Zurich. You can choose where you want the gold equivalent of your investment to be stored, and this should cater to those with a nervous disposition, who anticipate that gold may once again be confiscated if times get tough.

Investments can be made by a bank wire transfer into your BullionVault account, and the money can be wired back to your local bank just as easily. There is a $30 fee for the transfer, and generally the charges are quite reasonable, with a minimum $4 per month storage fee, regardless of the size of your gold holding.

A key concern that is driving the move toward digital gold is the massive spending being done to allay the problems of the financial breakdown. It seems inevitable that the multi-trillion dollar deficit spending will cause raging inflation just as soon as the effect is felt by the marketplace.

The advocates of the digital gold system maintain that it will be far more sustainable and constant for the future. Really, all they are doing is reestablishing a gold standard for currency and cutting out the complication of converting weights of gold into individual currency units, except when needed to interface with the real world. Given that recent history since the abandonment of any pretense at a gold standard has showed the weakness of allowing governments to regulate their money supply, they may have a point. All is not perfect, however, and you need to weigh the advantages and disadvantages against other ways of investing your money.

The advantages of digital gold include:

- The ease with which you can complete transactions from any Internet connected personal computer

- Much lower storage costs compared to individual storage

- The gold can be stored out of reach of your local government's jurisdiction, if you are concerned about seizure

- It may work out cheaper than conventional currency exchange when doing international business

Against those factors, you should weigh the disadvantages:

- You need to trust the private bank to always represent your interests and to allocate the right amount of gold to your account

- Unlike credit cards, you have no way of reversing a payment if the transaction goes sour

- You may be concerned about security and hacking into your account, and you need to assure yourself that the company's login procedure is sufficiently secure to avoid fraud

Since 1996, when digital gold first became an investment option, the virtual metal has allowed investors to easily complete transactions while having lower storage fees than traditional investment methods. However, the downsides of digital gold, being that the investment may not be as direct and as secure as other options, lead many investors to other methods, often related to the stock market.

CHAPTER FIVE

The Stock Market

It is not necessary for you to own or take delivery of physical gold to become involved in gold's success and staying power. There are many different ways to take part in an increase in value of gold without actually owning the metal. Some are more closely linked to the value of than others, and some may entail more risk, but consequently may give greater rewards — if successful.

The paper ways of investing in gold can be broken down into several different types of investments, some more speculative than others in terms of actually having the physical metal in your posses ion. If you feel more comfortable investing in stocks and shares than in the physical metal, there are a number of choices available for you, all of which have a chance of benefiting from an increase in the popularity of gold. After describing the different types of stock, you will learn what to look for in a stock investment, along with other ways in which the markets can be used to make a profit.

MINING STOCKS

The most obvious gold-related stocks are those concerned with mining, and these can be broken down into several different types, depending on how much gold the mining company produces. There are those companies that produce large portions of gold, as well as those companies who are simply exploring different areas and ways for mining the precious metal.

Major producing companies

There are a handful of industry giants who operate around the world. These are considered top-tier companies, and they have established reputations for success. Of all the mining companies, these offer the most conservative selection and the least risky shares in which to place your investment. It is generally agreed that the major producers are each responsible for more than 1 million ounces of gold each year. The largest of the producers is Barrick Gold, which operates out of Canada and is responsible for about 7 million ounces each year. Another major company in the U.S., Australia, Peru, Indonesia, Ghana, Canada, New Zealand, and Mexico is Newmont Mining, which is responsible for about 6 million ounces of consolidated gold. The next most important companies are based in South Africa. In total, there are about a dozen of these large companies.

Intermediate mining

For a little more excitement, you may wish to look into the stocks of a mid-tier company. These are often the up-and-coming mines, which have a large potential and may eventually become a top tier in company, but also have greater risk. The definition of this size of company is one that produces between 250,000 ounces and 1 million ounces a year. Again, there are several from South Africa, such as DRDGold, and there are also intermediate companies in Canada, Australia, and Britain. There are about the same number of producers in this size range as in the major range.

Exploratory mines

For investors who want to take an active interest in their money, the small producers give an excellent opportunity for a high-risk and high-potential return. Mining companies are not the same as the more familiar computer or retail companies in which you may invest, and some specialist knowledge is useful in determining which of these are sound enough to meet your criteria before investing your money.

These small companies typically are not proven producers. They may have had some success in the past, but generally they are looking to hit it big and find the perfect location for a productive mine. You will appreciate that if they succeed, these stocks may explode in value, but if they continue to explore without much success, then the value will fade away. These companies will typically only operate a single gold-producing property, as they will concentrate all their efforts into making it pay. There is no diversity in the event that the mine proves to have fewer reserves than expected, or has to shut down for some reason, meaning that stocks of these companies are subject to fall without warning, causing the investor to lose money.

The smallest companies include those who have yet to produce any gold, which for that reason are highly speculative companies. Some of these will have an expert opinion that supports a known amount of gold being present in their claim, and they are in the process of gearing up for production; others will have just made a discovery and be undertaking further tests to see whether it could be a commercial venture; and still others only have a drill rig and a lot of hope.

INVESTING IN MINING STOCKS

If you choose to invest in mining stocks, there are several things to keep in mind. First of all, you may find that the value of your mining stock will rise faster than the value of gold in a bull market, meaning the value of gold has increased for a prolonged period of time. This is because the increase in gold value, say a doubling in value, directly impacts the receipts, even though the overhead costs will not rise significantly. The percentage profit return is therefore greater than the mere increase in gold price. This is example of leveraging, or multiplying, the return on your investment.

This has not applied so much in recent years because of the rising costs of labor and the energy shortages. The underlying costs have also increased while the price of gold has gone up. A slight reduction in the price of gold may turn a profitable stock into one that loses, as this principle of leverage will work both ways.

The value of your stock may also be greatly affected by the economy. For example, there may be an increase in taxation, which will negate the mining company's expected profits, ultimately causing the value of your stock to decrease. There is even the threat that if the economy performs badly; for example, with the dollar continuing to lose value, the government could implement gold confiscation as a way of trying to consolidate debt, which would severely impact any stocks of companies involved in gold production.

On the other side, it is possible that a small investment can reap huge returns, especially if you have taken a risk with investment in intermediate or exploratory companies. Many companies fail to succeed in this business, but if you are lucky and shrewd with your selection, you can find that you make a good profit.

You should not restrict your choices to U.S.-based mining companies. Canada has a thriving gold mining industry, and if you make some investment with Canadian companies, you are diversifying a little against currency fluctuations. This way, your chances of having a successful investment portfolio will be greater than if you limit yourself to just one type of market and currency. You should look for mid-tier Canadian companies that are establishing a track record in gold production, but are still small enough to allow a fast rate of growth and consequently a good profit.

If you decide to diversify into Canadian mining stocks, you will find that the process is not much more difficult than investing in U.S. stocks. You simply have to find a broker who is licensed to do business in the Canadian market. The only issue you may find is that you have less choice of a discount broker, who carries out the regular buying and selling actions of a regular broker at a discounted commission rate, and you will have to pay a higher fee for the service of buying stocks.

When you are making your choice of which mining companies to invest in, you must consider several important points. First, the total amount of gold and precious metals that can be mined is relatively small and fixed because there are only so many places in the world where gold can actually be mined. Furthermore, it is not likely that many more places will be found that can provide a large production. The saying is that matter can be neither created nor destroyed, and although modern science may beg to differ with this as an absolute fact, it is true for normal conditions not involving nuclear devices.

Secondly, you need to review the potential or history of production of the company. Examine details of the production levels through the years and the costs of production. Review the company's latest annual report and any recent newsletters. If it is a U.S. company, you will be able to see the company earnings on a 10-K or 10-Q report. You may also ask for profiles of the major management personnel, so that you can confirm for yourself that they have good experience in the industry.

An important factor to calculate is the company's return on capital, which shows how much money the company is actually making for its shareholders. The fundamental formula involves calculating the net income after taxes have been deducted and comparing that with the capital invested, which should include not only shareholder money, but also money owed to the bank. The capital employed can be a cost to the company, and the net return should always be greater than the cost; otherwise, the company is effectively losing money all the time for its shareholders. For example, if a company's net income is $20,000 after taxes, and the capital invested is $30,000, the company is losing money for its investors.

The value of a mining company comes from three basic factors, which will affect the profitability and the return on your capital. The first of these is the possible growth in production. There are many aspects of this. With even a small increase in efficiency, there can be a marked effect on the return on investment. If the efficiency requires additional capital expenditure, then there is a balance to be struck between that expenditure and the amount of improvement that can be achieved. Sometimes production can grow, but it entails extracting ore of a lesser quality, which will need increased costs to extract the gold. This is a complex calculation, and information that you receive from the company on their ability to ramp up production should always be checked with the yardstick of realism, or with a professional opinion.

The second item affecting value of the company is the growth in reserves. The reserves are the amount of gold that is still in the ground. Of necessity, reserves are not proved until they are no longer reserves and have been mined, so again it is necessary to be cautious of relying too much on information that may be given to you. However, the questions to be asked include the quality of the reserves, which will affect the extraction cost, and how the quantity of the reserve has been determined. For instance, there may have been a program of drilling and analysis, or the reserves may be based more on the experience of the operators, which might be regarded as more speculative.

The company's value also depends ultimately on the cash flow that its operation can generate. You may not be able to pin this one down, as it depends on the stage of each mine. If the company is mainly in exploration, then the cash flow that can be achieved will only be an estimate. With an active mine, it is far easier to review the cash flow numbers and predict any changes. A mine that extracts more than one valuable resource is inherently able to generate greater cash flow than a single metal mine.

You need to strike a balance between the relative safety of a large producer with an established track record, and the potential for greater gain from an intermediate or even an exploratory company, with the associated high risks. If they have an active mine, consider how long it will remain active and the amount of gold that is still thought to be in the ground. If you are investing in a riskier prospect, you should be more aggressive in securing any profit. *In the trading advice offered in Chapter Six, you will see that you can set a "stop-loss" order to prevent losing too much on a stock.* As you will learn, this starts off well, but which may fluctuate in value. In all trading, but particularly if you are looking at risky prospects, be prepared to cut your losses quickly if the price does not go in the direction you desire.

Third, you should be aware of political considerations, as well as environmental factors. Environmental factors may include things like pollutants that are produced by mining. Such pollutants are by-products that occur with mining metals, such as sulfur and arsenic, which cause danger to the environment. Likewise, the chemicals used during mining are harmful pollutants, too. These environmental factors can contribute to some of the political factors associated with mining, which may play a role in whether you choose to invest in gold mining companies. Many investors will choose to spread their mining investments across different countries, particularly if some are subject to political upheaval, which could cause a problem to the company.

FUNDS AND DERIVATIVES

If you are interested in the gains that can be made from investing in mining companies but feel you do not have the time or expertise to select the stocks, you may find that mining funds are more suitable for you. Mining funds invest in gold mining stocks using money that investors put in the fund, but the funds also invest in other things, too, like bonds and securities. This way, an investment's success is not dependent on a stock alone. Typically, these are organized as mutual funds, so if you contribute money, you get a stake in all of the investments that make up the fund, allowing for easier diversification of your portfolio. If you are a conservative investor, you may find that a mutual fund gives you more peace of mind than direct investing in mining stocks.

Mutual funds

In essence, a mutual fund is a fund of money from many investors like you and is being managed by an investment firm and put into the market sector selected — in this case, mining. The money that you invest is added to the funds of other investors so that the mutual fund manager has control of a large amount that can be used to buy stocks that he or she selects. All you need to do is select which fund you wish to invest in, and then you rely on your chosen investment firm to pick investments that will make money.

You do not need much money to get started in a mutual fund, and you can add to your investment at any time. Most importantly, if you do not have the confidence or experience to select individual stocks, investing through a mutual fund means you have access to experienced advisors to make selections for you.

Depending on your needs, you can choose a mutual fund that makes conservative investments in large companies, or one that takes more risks and invests in growth stocks. In either case, your investment is diversified among several companies by the mutual fund manager, thus reducing the risk. As the manager's job is to watch the market and select stocks, you have the convenience of not having to follow each mining company yourself.

If you are new to investing in gold and precious metals, a mutual fund is a good way to start to take an interest, as you do not have to be an expert to achieve decent returns. Funds have done quite well for the majority of this century, even though they were affected by the recent financial crisis, as was just about every other market investment. Some funds you may be interested in are American Century Investment Global Gold (BGEIX), Fidelity Select Gold (FSAGX), and ASA Ltd. (ASA). You can find the latest information on these funds from your broker, or from an all-purpose investment Web site such as **www.MorningStar.com**. You should not restrict your choice to these three, as there are many others that are worthy of consideration, and you can obtain information about all of them from a reputable Internet source, such as MorningStar, Lipper & Company, and Value Line.

Your first consideration should be what type of investor you are, and how much of your capital you are prepared to put at risk. This will help you narrow down your fund selection. If you are averse to risk, you may still choose to become involved with a fund that is growth-oriented and inherently more of a chance. If you only put a small proportion of your capital into such a fund, you can have the excitement of following the ups and downs of the speculative and exploratory mining market without risking too much. *Risk is relative, and you will find more commentary on this later in Chapter Six, when trading for profit is discussed.*

Whether you are conservative or adventurous in your investments, you stand to profit from the current bullish trend in gold, and you can add more to your fund later as the market unfolds. Approach the matter of investing in a fund in a professional manner, considering your goals and objectives. It then becomes a business decision to decide on the fund company whose objectives seem the most in line with your own, and determining the amount you are prepared to risk. Here are some questions to ask yourself:

- **Why are you investing?** Is it to save money for your child's college fund, or simply for your retirement?

- **What is your investment time horizon?** In other words, how long do you have to invest? For short periods of time, low-risk investments are usually recommended. For periods that are around ten years or longer, investors tend to be more liberal.

- **Are you aiming for equity or income?** Some investors want to achieve both, as they seek investments in particular companies in addition to gaining income.

- **Do the rewards outweigh the risks?** The performance of your fund is important, but be sure to consider things like the fund's management and turnover rate.

In summary, there are several advantages to using mutual funds for at least part of your investment in gold and precious metal stocks. Remember, they are convenient because once you have decided on your fund, the rest of the work is up to the manager. A mutual fund also provides the opportunity for investors to rely on the work of a professional whose responsibility is to take care of day-to-day monitoring and administration of the investments. Secondly, by selecting the appropriate mutual fund, you can make sure that your money is invested in a way that matches your needs. Whether you need conservative, steady growth or are prepared to take more chances in the pursuit of higher rewards, there will be a fund to fit in your portfolio. Possibly the best feature of mutual funds, however, is the opportunity for diversification of your investment with even the smallest amount of money. Because they operate with pools of money from various investors, mutual funds have the ability to absorb a loss, which might have been critical to an individual investor. Even though one hopes the manager will not make mistakes in company selection, a stock that plummets will not devastate your portfolio. It is one way that you can try to partake of the investment potential in exploratory mining without risking total loss.

As with most investments, there are also some disadvantages to mutual funds that you must take into account before deciding whether they are the appropriate investment vehicle for your portfolio. The advantage that you have with a professional deciding on the company stocks to buy can also be seen as a disadvantage for investors who prefer to be hands-on. Some investors do not like the thought of leaving the fate of their money up to someone else. If you tend to think this way, then at least you should thoroughly analyze the fund you are considering and make sure they have a good reputation and history of success. Secondly, the mutual fund manager does not do the work for nothing, and there are fees associated with investing through a mutual fund. In brief, you should look for a fund that charges no more than the average for this type of mutual fund, and preferably one that has no load, or sales commission. Be sure that you check on all fees that will be asked before investing so that there are no surprises. You can calculate the cost of a mutual fund at **www.sec.gov/investor/tools/mfcc/mfcc-intsec.htm**, where the online calculator allows you to compare different types of mutual funds that have different fees and rates.

As part of your investigation of the mutual fund, you will be given a prospectus. This is an important document and explains the essence of the fund along with its historical performance. Mutual fund prospectuses must comply with many standards and contain information required by legislation. There are certain elements that every prospectus must provide, which include the fund's objective, the cost to invest, where the fund is or will be invested, and a standardized list of past performance. You will find that because of the regulations, much of the information is expressed in the same terms and can be easily compared between different funds.

Exchange-traded funds

Exchange-traded funds (ETFs) are another way of investing in mining companies, similar to mutual funds. They are a comparatively recent invention and are proving extremely popular. The difference with an ETF is that it is traded like stock, on a market. An ETF is not managed in the same way as a mutual fund, with a manager buying and selling stocks on the basis of his or her research; an ETF normally contains a fixed set of securities, a basket of commodities, and the price of the ETF reflects the movement of the security prices. In this way, they are more of a trading vehicle than the mutual fund, even though they can be held for the long-term because of the built in diversity. If you see a general downturn in the market for gold, it is equally easy for you to sell your ETFs on the market and avoid losses.

As with mutual funds, your money goes into a pool with money from other investors, and this allows you to enjoy the diversity of investment in many different stocks. An advantage over mutual funds is that there are far fewer costs, as you do not have to pay for an expert manager to monitor the shareholding. You will simply pay fees to trade the ETFs. Because of this arrangement, they are much more flexible than mutual funds for buying and selling your interest.

The disadvantage of using ETFs is that the performance is directly tied to the industry that the ETF is based in. You are not getting any additional performance, such as that which manager might be expected to give to a fund. You are also subject to the market fluctuations in your chosen sector. If the market sector is promising, such as gold appears to be, then this is not necessarily a problem.

ETFs that invest in gold companies include the iShares® COMEX Gold Trust (IAU) and the PowerShares DB Gold Fund (DGL).

If you are interested in trading in the values of the actual metals of gold and silver, rather than just trading on the companies that are involved with precious metals, then you should look into another form of ETF. The ticker symbol for the gold ETF is GLD, and for the silver ETF is SLV. The stated aim of these ETFs is to reflect the price of the metals, but this is not necessarily the same thing as owning the metals. They have the advantage that they are easily traded, unlike buying and selling the physical materials.

Though the ETF is useful if you are trading, you should not consider it if you want to invest in gold. One of the points of owning gold is that it is outside the financial system, which has proved itself to be weak and subject to failure in various ways. If you buy an ETF, you are buying what is essentially a stock within the financial system. In fact, the ETF is a share in a trust that is owned by a bank, and the bank may or may not have sufficient gold to cover all the interest in the ETF. Even if it does have enough gold to cover the interest, the gold is in the name of the bank — not in your name.

The gold and silver ETFs may arguably be called examples of "digital gold," which was covered in a Chapter Four. However, as they are more closely related to the stock market, they are included here. As a reminder, there are also digital bullion trading exchanges available, which are private trading systems on which customers purchase and trade in metals. The exchanges store the metals that are being traded and guarantee that all the investments are covered by the value of the gold and other metals stored. All trading must pass through the Web site, and not through your broker. When you use this system, you are not trading on the commercial market but are trading with other customers of the trading exchange, so there may be some differences in price from the open market.

Futures

Many people are concerned when they think about trading futures, as they have heard tales of how people have lost everything by trading futures badly. While this section cannot be a complete guide to how to trade futures profitably, it should demystify the topic and show you the possibilities for profit if you add futures to your trading armory. It will also show you the areas that you need to be especially careful about if you want to preserve your capital.

Futures derive their value because of the assets they represent, sometimes called the underlying assets or simply the "underlying." They are available on virtually any commodity and on many different shares and indices, and the market for futures is expanding wherever the need arises. A future, or more correctly a futures contract, is a contract for buying and selling something in the future. The something and the quantity of it is specified, the price is specified, and the date of the transaction is specified. When you trade futures, you are simply trading the contract, buying and selling the responsibility to complete the transaction on the agreed date — you are not actually buying and selling the commodity. To be successful trading futures, you need to develop your concept of risk versus return and assess where you think the price of the underlying will go in the future, and with what uncertainty.

Although futures, because of their nature, are regarded as highly speculative, that is only one view of the transaction. They can be used to remove risk from an investment and from business. For instance, if a cereal manufacturer wants to be sure of a supply of cereal for future production, they can buy a futures contract from a broker, which guarantees they can obtain the quantity they want at a certain date in the future. The price is agreed when the contract is bought, and the cereal manufacturer knows exactly what costs they will have to pay. Regardless of the weather, crop diseases, or other problems, the manufacturer can be assured of the supply at a set price. This totally removes the risk, albeit by agreeing to pay what may possibly be a higher price than the market price on the date in question, if the harvest has been good.

On the other side of the equation, the farmer may seek to agree the futures contract so that he or she is assured of a minimum price for their crop. In that way, the farmer knows that it will be worthwhile to buy the seed and fertilizer, and tend the crop while it grows. Certainly, the farmer is exposed to some risk of crop failure and will have to satisfy the contract even if the growth is not sufficient. No one is in a better position to make that evaluation and decide on the level of risk to take than the farmer, who may decide, for example, to commit half of his or her expected crop to the futures contract receiving a higher price. If the harvest is good, the farmer can sell the remainder at the lower market price, but if there is a problem with the growing season, he or she will still hope to meet the futures commitment. So both parties to the contract can approach it as an advantage, which takes away the uncertainty of the business.

Futures trading is highly organized, with standardized quantities, delivery dates, and quality standards. Because of the opportunity to leverage the power of your money, futures contracts are heavily traded by speculators and are often settled in cash, rather than by taking delivery of the underlying. The volume of trading means that the market is extremely efficient, and the futures exchange works well to discover a true price for each contract. Futures prices are available around the world, so international trade is easily facilitated, for example, by Russia selling wheat to the U.S.

From a practical point of view, you should note that the gains and losses of futures contracts cancel out. That is, if one trader gains from the contract, the trader on the other side of the contract loses the same amount, neglecting any other trading charges. If the first trader takes a contract to buy gold for $1,000 per ounce in September, and the spot price at expiration is $1,100, he or she makes $100 per ounce, and the trader on the other side of the contract will lose $100 per ounce. If gold is trading for $900 per ounce in September, the first trader is still committed to pay $1,000 per ounce, losing $100, but meaning the seller makes $100 per ounce. There are many combinations of trades that can be made to hedge the outcome, particularly if the trader sees that there may be a losing position coming up — but the basic principle is as outlined, and your gain is someone else's loss, or vice versa. If you see that your futures contract is going to be out of the money, you can even sell it to someone else and take a small loss rather than holding onto it until the end, when you may be facing a bigger loss. The person buying it from you, of course, is gambling that the price will go back up.

If you are inexperienced, then it is likely that a more experienced trader will manage to take advantage of you, which is why, as a novice, you are particularly open to losses when you trade futures. The way around this is to commit the time and energy to learn more about the markets you are interested in so that you can become a knowledgeable trader, better at making your selections than the novices who are just starting out. Many of the underlying goods will be familiar to you, if you have ever taken part in the markets, and as futures depend on the prices of the underlying, you will be using the same skills you acquired previously in figuring whether the price will go up or down. Here is a list of some of the items that you can trade on the futures market:

- Precious metals, including gold, silver, platinum, and palladium
- Base metals, including copper, zinc, nickel, tin, lead, and aluminum
- Plastics and lumber
- Energy, including crude oil and gas
- Grains, including corn, wheat, and soybeans
- Meats, including cattle and pork
- Other foods, including sugar and coffee
- Financial instruments, including bonds and Treasury notes
- Indices, including the NASDAQ and the Dow Jones Industrial Average
- Stocks
- Currencies, including the dollar, the euro, and British pounds (although the pound is not commonly used)

There are four main groups of people that are involved in trading futures: exchanges, speculators, hedgers, and regulators. The typical investor would fall under the "speculators" category, and that is the one focused on here. As an investor, you would be looking to make a profit and not be so concerned with the underlying. A speculator's goal is to benefit from the ups and downs of the markets. As mentioned, many of the futures traders have the same motivation, and perhaps as little as 15 percent or less are involved in the market expecting to receive delivery of the commodity. In fact, some of the futures cannot even be settled by a delivery. For example, if you have a futures contract on stock indices, then you will not expect to receive a range of stocks from the different companies that comprise the index. This contract will always be settled with money.

Futures contracts are always associated with a specific delivery date, and that is standardized across the industry. Every precious metal that is traded in the futures market will comply with the dates, which can be found online at **www.nymex.com**, the Web site for the New York Mercantile Exchange (NYMEX). The precious metals that are best for trading futures are gold, silver, platinum, and palladium, and you can find more details and specific information on the Web site.

In order to take on a futures contract, you are required to provide a margin, which is a deposit, to cover the broker against risk. You do not have to pay for the goods before delivery; in practice, if you are trading for speculation, you will never pay for the commodity, but you are required to lodge a percentage of the contract price so that you can make the trade. Often, the margin deposit is no more than 20 percent of the entire contract. This leverages your investment and is key to why futures contracts can be so lucrative — because you are anticipating a financial gain — but also dangerous for the unaware.

You see, if you were to buy gold for $1,000 per ounce, expecting it to increase in value to $1,100 per ounce next month, you would invest $1,000 per ounce and expect to make a 10 percent profit. If, on the other hand, you took out a futures contract with the same expectations, it would cost you a little over $200 per ounce, and you would still make $100 per ounce, giving you a nearly 50 percent return. On the downside, the leverage will work against you if you choose the wrong direction, so you will lose a far greater percentage of your money. You can even lose all of your money and be left owing your broker more, and this is the basis for the dangerous reputation of futures.

It can also be a little more complicated than that, and certainly more complex than straight trading in stocks or commodities. Each day, your broker will "mark to market" your contracts, which means that he or she values them based on the latest prices. If the price is going up, then he or she will credit your account with the increase, and everyone is happy. If the price is going down, and the margin in your account is no longer sufficient to cover the possible loss, then you may receive a "margin call" from your broker, which is when your broker asks you to deposit more funds in your account. If you ignore this call, the broker is entitled to liquidate your position, which means you may miss out if there was a subsequent gain. In fact, the broker is not even obligated to give you a margin call, but is allowed to protect his or her own interests against your losses.

Above, the example of costs was given on a per-ounce basis. But, as originally mentioned, futures contracts are standardized, with standard amounts in each contract. The contract size for gold is 100 ounces, and with the price of gold around $1,000 per ounce at the time of writing this book, a futures contract will be for $100,000 worth of gold. Even buying a futures contract on margin could be too expensive for many investors. Because of this, the exchanges have created something called a mini contract, which involves a much smaller amount of gold. In the case of the NYMEX, the contract size is 50 ounces, and in the Chicago Mercantile Exchange (CME), the size is even smaller, at 33.2 ounces. The actual margin that your broker wants to charge you will vary from broker to broker, so you will need to check and see how much money you need in your account to enter one of these futures contracts, but clearly they are much more affordable than the full-size contracts.

Managed futures accounts

If you would like to invest on the futures market because you want to have some commodity exposure in your portfolio, then you may wish to consider opening a managed futures account. As the name implies, managed futures accounts involve trading with futures that are managed for you by a professional advisor. It is specifically geared to the investor who wants the growth potential of the futures market, but still wants to accept a certain amount of risk. You will find there is a minimum amount required to open an account, and this may be as much as $50,000.

As with trading futures for yourself, this involves significant exposure and should only be considered if you are in the position of having a large portfolio and want some exposure to the futures market. Managed futures, and even mini futures contracts, are not really for the small investor, who may want a more secure and less volatile place to put his or her savings.

A managed futures account will be invested for you by a registered money manager, also known as a commodity trading advisor (CTA). The body that controls registration is called the Commodity Futures Trading Commission (CFTC), which has a

Web site at **www.cftc.gov**. Though registration ensures a certain level of competency, you will want to independently examine the individual CTA's record and references to see how well they operate.

You should ask to review the track record and methods used by anyone whom you are considering opening a managed futures account with. Their track record should show not only the average gains, but also the amount that an account can be expected to fluctuate when held in their care. There are several different methods used by CTAs, and they may choose to use one or more of them. Some will go long only, which means they are buying in the expectation that the security will increase in value, and some prefer the short positions, which seek to find weakness in order to profit. Others combine both these approaches by trading a spread, which is a combination of long and short that reduces risks.

In many ways, a managed futures account is similar to any other managed fund, such as a mutual fund or hedge fund. You will be able to see what positions the manager has taken, and keep an eye on the progress of your account. Because of a potential conflict of interest, the money manager does not work on commission from the trades, so he or she is recompensed with a percentage of the account performance rather than on a flat or standard commission fee.

Like other managed accounts, you do not have to be involved in day-to-day decisions on what futures to trade. A CTA will be able to trade on all types of futures contracts, not just gold and precious metals, and you may find that this diversification is more available in keeping with your investing goals. You can expect professional management of your account and results that are better than you could achieve as a neophyte.

Options

While futures entail the obligation for the contract to be settled, you may also choose to trade options, which just give you the choice of buying or selling a commodity at some time in the future. An option is just what the name suggests: It is a contract for some set time in the future for the commodity to be bought or sold, but performance of the contract is optional. If you have an option that will not make you money, you have no obligation to go through with the transaction. This immediately cuts out the downside of futures by taking away the obligation to complete the contract at whatever price was agreed. You will only "exercise" your option if by doing so you are going to make money.

Once again, you can get options to cover a wide range of underlying assets, just as with futures. Often options are associated with buying shares, and a standard option in this case is for 100 shares. But options are available based on most financial instruments and assets; you can even buy an option on a futures contract, meaning that as an investor, you have the right to buy or sell your futures contract at a designated price.

A call option is a contract that allows the option buyer to purchase the underlying commodity at a set price on or before the expiration date of the option. In this, the simplest of cases, the buyer expects the price to go up above the set price, which is called the "strike price" of the option. Exercising the option at the set price, the commodity will be bought at less than the future market price. As a side note, if you buy options in Europe, you will find they are slightly different: In Europe, you may only exercise the option at the expiration date, and not before.

Note that you need to buy an option — that is, the option contract costs you money that does not go toward the commodity. The more likely the option will end up making money, the more expensive it is likely to be. If the strike price is very high, then it is unlikely that the option will make money and will cost very little. If you are buying an option, the most you can lose is the cost of the option, if the commodity does not rise in price as you had hoped.

Again, considering only this most simple of cases, there are several outcomes for the option buyer:

- The underlying asset goes down in value and is less than the strike price. When the expiration date comes, the option expires worthless, and you have lost the money you paid for it.

- The underlying asset goes up in value, to a little more than the strike price. You exercise the option before the expiration date and make money on the difference between the price when exercised and the strike price. This offsets some of the cost of the option that you have already paid.

- The underlying asset goes up in price a lot. You again exercise the option, at a time of your choosing before the expiration date, and make money on the difference between the price when exercised and the strike price. This time the money more than covers the original cost of the option, and you make a profit on the whole deal.

- Rather than waiting for one of the above results, you can also sell the option contract you bought. Depending on how the underlying asset is performing, you may get more money than you paid for the option, or you may get less. You can use this method to reduce your loss if you believe that the option will expire worthless.

In summary, if you choose to buy a call option, you stand to gain whenever the underlying assets rise in value sufficiently above the strike price. There is no theoretical limit to how high the asset could go, so your gains are not restricted. If the underlying asset falls in value, your losses are limited to the price you paid for the option. As you can see, this method provides a much safer, limited risk than using futures.

The other type of option contract in general use is called the put option. This is the opposite of the call option, and it gives the buyer of the option the rights to sell an asset for a set price. The buyer would be expecting the price to fall, allowing him or her in theory to buy it on the open market and exercise the option, forcing the option writer to buy it at a higher price, thus making the buyer a profit. In practice, the commodity would not need to be bought, and the option could be settled in cash for the difference in price.

The option contract will again cost money, which may be lost. If the strike price is close to the current price, and the market is bearish, or declining, then the option is likely to make money and will be expensive. If the strike price is much less than the current price, or it is a bull market, then the put option can be bought quite cheaply. The possible outcomes for the put option buyer are:

- The underlying asset goes up in value and is more than the strike price. The expiration date arrives, and the option expires worthless. The cost of the option is lost.

- The underlying asset goes down to a little below the strike price. When the option is exercised, the buyer makes a little money, but not as much as the option cost, leaving a small loss overall.

- The underlying asset drops well below the strike price. Exercising the option makes a profit, even after deducting the original price of the option.

- As with the call option, the put option buyer may sell the option contract to another buyer, resulting in a small profit or loss.

As with the call option, the worst that can happen to the put option buyer is that they lose the cost of the option at the expiration date. The best that can happen is that the bottom drops out of the price, which will result in a large profit.

So far in discussing options, life has been good, and the worst that can happen is that the trader loses the money paid for the option. Some people will trade in this way, with a limited and defined downside on entering the trade and a much less restricted possible upside. There is another side to options, which involves slightly more risk but can provide better returns, and that is being an option writer — in other words, an option seller.

Consider now the case of an option writer for a call option. The option writer, who plays the role of the "seller" in this transaction, receives the buyer's money for the option up front, and this can be put to any other purpose desired. The writer then waits, perhaps up to the expiration date, before knowing what other commitments may be involved. Here are the possible outcomes:

- The underlying asset goes down in value and is less than the strike price. The option expires worthless, and you keep the money you were paid for the option with no further commitment.

- The underlying asset goes up in value, above the strike price. The buyer executes the option, and you must sell the underlying asset at the agreed price. This may involve buying the asset at the market price, or you may already own it.

Similarly, you can be an option writer for a put option. The outcomes will be similar, but vice versa to the call option.

There are a couple of common strategies used to make money with options, but managing risk is perhaps the best way that you can make money using options. The first is called the covered call. This involves writing a call option for stocks that you already own. Remember that an option typically covers 100 shares, so you can write or sell a call for every 100 shares of the stock you own. This strategy is called a covered call because the option you sell is covered by your shareholding.

When you sell the call option, you take on the obligation to sell your stock at the strike price if the trade goes against you. However, you get the immediate income of the premium paid for the call option, and if the option is never exercised, this is pure profit. When you sell the call, you must use your judgment of the strike price that will not be reached in the time available so that you do not have to sell your shareholding. If the markets work well for you, you can get a regular income selling another call option each time the expiration date of the previous one comes around. The worst that can happen is that you are forced to sell your shares at a price below the current market price, but above where you originally bought them.

Another way of making an income is to write a put option for a share that you would like to own. If the market price hits the strike price, you will have the obligation of buying the shares at that price. You can use this strategy when you are watching a share, wanting to buy it if only it would become cheap enough. For example, say you have decided that XYZ Mining, which is currently trading at $30, would be worth buying if it dropped to $25. You can sell a put option with a strike price of $25, one option for every hundred shares you want to buy. Thus, the put option allows you to buy the share when it reaches the price of $25, but does not force you to buy it if the price does not go that low.

There are two possible outcomes:

- The price of the shares will drop to $25 or less, and you will be forced to buy them at $25. As this is what you wanted to do in the first place, then you should be happy — you may need to ignore the fact that you could have bought them even cheaper, if they have dropped further.

- The price of the shares stays above $25, and the put option is not exercised.

In either case, you receive the premium paid for the option. In the first case, you can consider this as discounting the price that you paid for the shares you want to own. In the second case, this is pure income, and you can write another put option after the expiration date of the first, assuming that you still wish to own the shares.

There are many more strategies available, with names like collars and straddles, and these are more specialized. You will find details of them in any course on options. By knowing how futures, options, and exchange-traded funds work, you will be in a better position to gauge which investment will bring you the most profit.

CHAPTER SIX

Trading for Profit

P revious discussions have focused on holding stocks and bonds for the long haul, with futures and options being available for the prospect of short-term profit. If you are prepared to put time into it, it is possible to achieve higher returns by trading, which simply means that you buy and sell the equities, securities, and derivatives instead of just holding onto a good pick, which is more commonly known as investing.

Trading can take place on a variety of time frames, depending on your propensity for risk and time available. Most people have heard about day trading, which is when a trader buys and sells securities all day long. This is an intense occupation and is a fast-paced way of either getting very rich or becoming poor. But trading can also take place on other time frames. A popular way to trade is using end-of-day (EOD) figures and charts, reviewing your positions in the evening after work, and deciding on your broker orders for the next day. Trading covers the range of buying and selling securities within a reasonably short time frame, which is up to a few weeks.

Within that time frame, there is little chance for fundamental factors to have much influence on the price. A trader may pay some cursory attention to the company's fundamentals to avoid being taken by surprise with some underlying but not yet common knowledge revelation about the company's performance. Sometimes the fundamentals will reveal a reason why a stock price can move rapidly in a short time. At other times, there may be little clue that the price is about to change — for example, if a mining company announces a major new find or a new location to mine. Without a crystal ball, it may be impossible to anticipate these times, and thus it is impossible to gauge a possible price change. Most of the time traders rely on technical analysis rather than fundamental analysis to decide when to buy and sell. Technical analysis attempts to anticipate the many fluctuations in price during normal trading periods so that equities can be bought and sold appropriately to make a profit, but it does not seek to anticipate fluctuations made by things like new discoveries.

There are several important points that you should note if you decide to try to make a profit from trading, whether in mining and related stocks or in other markets.

First of all, most of the time trading is a zero-sum exercise. By that, it means that the amount that you make in profit is the amount another trader or investor loses. Barring big moves that are caused by a shift in the fundamentals, over the time frame that trading takes place, the underlying value of the stock does not vary much. The price fluctuations happen because of different perceptions of the value, and that is subjective. Your task is to be smarter than the other traders so that you come out ahead.

Secondly, most people who start trading give up within six months, as they do not make consistent profits. To some extent this point follows from the first. It seems that on average, half the people trading should make a profit, and half will lose. This ratio becomes biased in favor of losing when you take into account the fact that there are costs associated with trading that must be met. These costs include brokers' commissions, and quite possibly software and data feed costs. By themselves, these would not account for the more than 80 percent of traders who fail to make a profit and give up. But you must also factor in that those few traders who do make a profit have probably become very experienced and are making a living at it. It may hurt to take the losses that the losing traders have, but most of them would not amount to enough money to live on. Ergo, there must be more losing traders than winning traders for the amounts to balance.

If you find this analysis somewhat depressing, and it is making you reconsider your decision to try trading, take heart from the fact that it means there are always novice traders with new money in the markets making mistakes, and when you become experienced, you will have a great advantage over them. Until you are in a position to have this advantage over the novice buyers, however, you may want to consider counsel from a financial adviser.

GOING SHORT

Before getting into the details of what to look for in successful trading, a common problem needs to be addressed. Many people are drawn into trading under the assumption that advertisements are true: You can make money trading whether the market is going up or down.

It is true that you can make money whether stocks go up or down in price. You usually need to decide which way you think they are going and place your trade accordingly. There are a few methods available that allow you to profit whether the stock goes up or down — as long as it moves a certain distance from its original price — or to profit if the stock does not move more than a certain distance from its original price, but these methods are a little too complex for the purposes of this explanation.

It is fairly easy to understand how you can profit when a stock goes up in price. You buy some shares of the stock, or in the jargon, "go long" on the stock, and when the stock goes up in price, you can sell those shares for a profit. You pay a fee to your broker when you buy and when you sell, but as long as the shares went up enough, the profits will cover the fee and give you some spending money.

Many people have difficulty understanding how you can do the opposite process in trading — making a profit when the stock goes down in price. But the idea is simple. Instead of buying the stock, you sell the stock, or in the jargon, "go short" on the stock. When the stock goes down in price, you simply buy it and profit by the difference, less commission again.

It is a simple idea, but the actual execution confuses many people. In practice, you need not worry about being confused, as any complication "going short" requires is taken care of by your broker, leaving you free to choose the stocks that will make you money. The confusion arises because in shopping and other buying and selling, you normally would not consider, or be able to sell something, before you bought it. Therefore, there seems to be a disconnect between what is possible in the real world and what traders do.

"Short selling" is a powerful concept, and you do yourself no favors if, as a trader, you are not comfortable with it and try to avoid it. Consider, for instance, the typical movements of a stock price. It often seems to take a long time to build up the price, only for it to drop quickly when there is a setback. If you do not "short" stocks, you can miss out on some substantial profits if the market is fluctuating.

Short selling should not seem so strange if you think about other comparable situations in life. For instance, when you buy a car, it is frequently the case that the dealer does not have the exact color or precise options that you want. When the dealer promises to deliver the car that you want, he or she is selling short — that is, selling something that he or she does not possess, with the earnest intention of finding and supplying it later to satisfy the contract.

The actual mechanics by which your broker provides the short-selling facility require that the shares are "borrowed" from another source so that they can be sold; then, they are replaced when you close out the trade and buy the shares to be handed back. This is called "buying to cover." The broker may borrow the shares from another client who owns them, or sometimes take them from the broker's own in-house supply of shares.

The essence of the broker's task is to make the temporary loss of the shares from the client's account transparent. The client should have no clue that anything has been done with them. To this end, there are certain things that the broker must do. If the shares are due a dividend — meaning a portion of the company's earnings — while they are shorted, then a dividend of the correct amount must be paid. This would be deducted from your account, if you are holding the short position. If the client should decide that he or she wants to sell the shares, then the broker will try to "borrow" the shares from another client to provide the replacement. It can happen that there are no more shares to borrow, in which case the broker is allowed to close out your trade by buying the shares at market, so that the client is made whole, regardless of the current price. This is unusual, but a necessary ultimate step if no other course exists.

Generally, as mentioned above, none of this will matter to you, as the short sale followed by buying to cover to close out the trade upon your instruction will be handled smoothly by the broker. The fact that these actions need to be taken explains why short selling is a little more limited in scope than buying long. Some stocks cannot be sold short, as the market in them is not large enough to allow the process — simply meaning there are no shares available to borrow.

There are some pitfalls in short selling, but they are mainly for the broker to avoid. A broker might take a chance and not borrow shares to cover the short sale. This is not an acceptable practice, but that does not mean that it does not happen, whether by chance or intent. Effectively, the broker would be taking the opposite trade to yours and betting that the shares would rise in value, which would mean that you had to pay him or her when you closed the trade.

Finally, an interesting note about short selling: Just as when investors buy shares, there may come a point at which many decide they have made a sufficient amount and sell for a profit, causing the price to drop back by supply and demand, so the situation may apply to short selling. The difference with short selling is that you can anticipate the unfolding of these events more clearly. When many people have gone short on a stock, and the price has fallen as expected, then there may be a rush of buying to cover the short positions, which causes the price to go up again. The fact is that the short positions must be covered at some time, and shares must be bought — that is the difference from the example of the long position, where no one particularly needs to sell. So if many people have shorted a stock, correctly anticipating a price drop, then it is likely that the fall in price will not continue indefinitely because they all have to buy to cover. If the price starts rising because of buying to cover, that will encourage more short sellers to vacate their positions. Thus, you will find that short selling can have an influence on the way the price fluctuates.

TECHNICAL ANALYSIS

Technical analysis, although it sounds like it might be highly mathematical, is actually as much an art as a science. Certainly, there are many numbers involved, but these are easily dealt with by computer programs, so they require no particular mathematical ability. The purpose of technical analysis is to decide which way a stock price will go in the short-term, and this means it is dependent more on the psychology of the mass of traders than it is on any particular numbers.

The analyst will look at the information that is available, including historical prices and amount of buying and selling, or volume, and attempt to project into the future what the information of the past can foretell. One of the early lessons that you learn as a trader is that the market is bigger than anyone, and it will do what it wants. You must discard the mindset that says the price "should" go up or down, based on your analysis. At the end of the day, you are seeking to put the odds in your favor, and there is no compulsion for any particular prediction to turn out to be correct. Often, the successful traders only predict 70 percent of the moves correctly, and it is even possible to be wrong more often than you are right and still make a profit, as the extent of your losses should be limited by good money management.

One of the fundamental ideas behind technical analysis — and the reason that it provides some help in trading — is that people are people and tend to react in the same way each time they are faced with the same set of circumstances. If history does not repeat itself, that is probably because you missed out on one vital difference when doing your analysis. In the nature of the markets, there are cycles in pricing that provide some predictability. It usually works out best to follow the trend, whether the price is increasing or falling, until the trend fails and the price direction changes.

Charts

Most traders who use technical analysis depend on studying charts of the price over time. There are numerous free resources on the Internet to compile stock charts, and you will usually find that your broker has facilities to assist you, too. You will find an example of what you can expect at **www.stockcharts.com**. On the chart, you will find that the y-axis, going vertically, represents the price, and the x-axis, horizontally along the bottom, has the time and date. This timescale can take many different values, depending on what type of trader you are. The day trader will typically look at the minute-by-minute moves of a price, and the end-of-day trader will have a scale of days, but there are selections from several minutes through hours, weeks, and months available for different purposes. Here is a sample daily chart for gold (GLD) as of 2009:

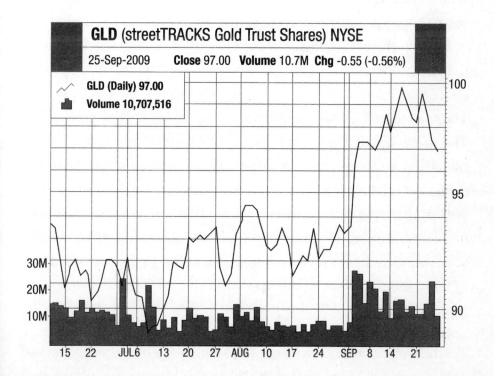

You can see that the price was just below $90 in the early part of July 2009 and touched $100 in September. GLD is the symbol for SPDR Gold Trust, an ETF that buys gold bullion, a metal that comes in its primary form of value. Each share of SPDR, also known as Standard & Poor's Spider, is equal to one-tenth of the S&P index. This is an interesting ETF to watch, particularly as the billionaire John Paulson — who runs the hedge fund firm Paulson & Co. — increased his fund's holding in the ETF in the first quarter of 2009. The hedge fund now owns nearly 9 percent of the ETF.

This is an example of a simple line chart, with the black line tracking gold's price throughout the displayed months. The gray bars along the bottom show you the volume of trading on each day, with a scale on the left of the chart that reads 10M, 20M, 30M, and so on. For example, there were nearly 30 million shares traded on one day at the beginning of September, after several weeks of less than 10 million shares being traded per day. You can also see the effect that this had on the price, which rapidly moved upward. Thus, as fewer shares were traded, the price of gold increased. The mere fact that there is a large volume of shares traded does not command whether the price goes up or down, or stays the same, but on days with large volume being traded, whatever happens is usually significant, as by definition it represents the view of a large number of traders. In this case, the rising price, which was supported by a large volume of trading in those early days of September, has set a new level, and the price has not dropped back down.

To understand a little more regarding how the line chart is developed, you should know that the line chart is actually a plot of the closing price for the stock on each day. This is not the only information available, however, and technical analysts will often use price charts that show more price information for the stock. The data values that are generally available include the opening price at the start of the day, the closing price or last price paid, the highest price traded in the day, and the lowest price of the day. These are four different price levels, although sometimes they may be the same; for instance, the last price of the day may also be the highest price of the day.

There are two common ways to view this information. One is called the Western bar chart and, until about 20 years ago, this was the main price chart used by traders. The other form of chart, which many people think expresses the sentiment of the market more clearly, is called a candlestick chart, and this has been used by the Japanese for centuries. Steve Nison is credited with discovering this technique and introducing it to Western traders. Here are examples of each, using the same period as the line chart:

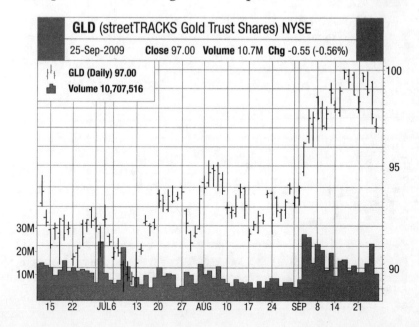

GLD (streetTRACKS Gold Trust Shares) NYSE

25-Sep-2009   Close 97.00   Volume 10.7M   Chg -0.55 (-0.56%)

GLD (Daily) 97.00
Volume 10,707,516

The bar chart, pictured above, has a vertical line or bar for each time period — in this case, each day — and the bottom of the bar represents the lowest price that the share sold for during the day. The top of the bar, as you might guess, is set at the highest price for the day. The price when the market opened is shown by the little line on the left of the bar, which is called a tick, and the price in the market closed is the tick on the right of the bar. Sometimes on a bar chart, you will notice there are bars that are colored red. These bars signal that the stock's value has gone down over this period. Essentially, a stock's decreasing value can also be shown by the dash on the right, which represents the closing price of the stock, and being lower than the dash on the left, which represents the stock's value when the market opened that day.

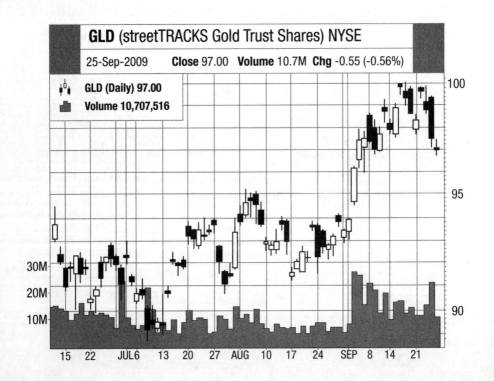

The previous candlestick chart is that most frequently used by traders, but it shows exactly the same information as the bar chart above it. They both have the extra values for each day's trading.

For the candlestick chart, immediately above, the vertical line stretches from the lowest price to the highest price of the day, as with the bar chart. The rectangle on the bar, which is either black or white, stretches between the opening price and the closing price. If the closing price was higher than the opening price, then the rectangle is white. The bottom of the rectangle is the opening price, and the top of the rectangle is the closing price. If the closing price was less than the opening price, then the rectangle is black (some charts will use red instead of black). The bottom of the rectangle is the closing price, and at the top of the rectangle is the opening price. Sometimes candlestick charts are shown in color, and by convention green is used instead of white for a bullish candle; red is used instead of black when the price has fallen over the day.

The advantages of the candlestick chart over the bar chart are that the opening and closing prices are much more easily seen, and it is obvious at a glance whether the prices are trending upward with mainly white rectangles, or bodies, or downward with black. With the bar chart, on the other hand, it takes a little more than just a glance to tell the where the prices started and ended for the day, as you only have a small tick to determine the price range and rise or fall of the stock.

Price trends

One of the first pieces of information, which you can often see when looking at a price chart, is the overall trend of the price:

whether it is going up or down, or whether it is staying around the same level. Traders often quote the advice that you should "let the trend be your friend," which means that your trades should be selected to go in the same direction as the trend of the price. This is decent advice, although there are times when you may wish to trade for the opposite result — for example, when you decide that the price is having a temporary pullback in a bullish, or upward, run. Also, prices do not trend all the time, so if you only trade with a trend, you will find your money is out of the market fairly often. This is not always a bad thing, as one of the mistakes of novice traders is to think that they always need to have their money in the market and working for them, even if they cannot identify a good prospect and settle for second-best, which is more likely to fail.

Trends can be quantified and drawn on a price chart, which gives the trader a visual clue to the future direction of the security. To understand the usefulness of this, you need to first comprehend the idea of support and resistance when applied to charts. Support and resistance are levels of price, which are maintained by the demand and supply of the market.

Specifically, support is a level of price below which it seems the security is unlikely to go. The support serves as a floor for the stock, which stops the prices from going below a certain level. When the security price reaches down to the support level, it seems to bounce off it, moving back up. Sometimes the price will fluctuate up and down several times, in each case stopping its fall at the same level, which confirms that the support is holding. In supply and demand terms, when the security price falls to this

level, the demand from traders who see it as good value over-
comes any bearish (downward) trend.

The opposite of this is resistance, which occurs when there is
new selling that emerges to hinder a price that is on the rise.
Sometimes the price of a security will push upward, only to
seem to hit a glass ceiling. Again, the price may approach the resistance level several times and not be able to go through it, and
the more times it does this, the more you can have confidence in
the resistance holding. Looked at in simple terms, the resistance
level can be thought of as a price at which many people would
like to sell and take a profit. With a large supply of the stock on
sale, there is no reason for the price to go higher, so the level
holds as the maximum price that will be attained. Support and
resistance lead to the classic price chart where the security is
going "sideways," bouncing up and down between the bound-
aries of support and resistance.

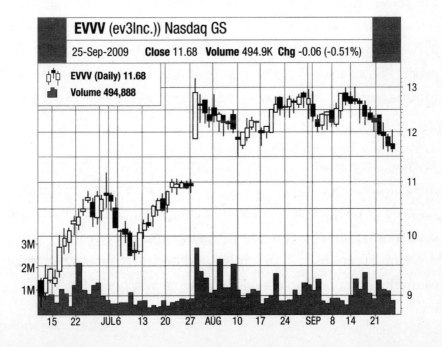

Here is a chart of ev3 Inc., which manufactures medical products, demonstrating sideways movement since the end of July. You can see that support is at 11.5, which the price has touched twice, and resistance is at 13.0 — the top of the chart, also recognized as the ceiling — which has been touched several times and is firmly established. Note that the slight overshoot on July 28 is not significant, as this is not an exact science.

The fact that you can identify support and resistance on a chart does not mean that these values are immutable. The market will do what it wants to do, and sometimes the price will keep going up past resistance to set new highs. When this happens, it is called a breakout, as the price is breaking out of the restricted range it has been trading in.

A curious occurrence, which has been frequently observed and is therefore a principal of technical analysis, is that after a breakout, the previous resistance becomes a support level. (If the breakout was downward, the support becomes resistance). The chart above demonstrates the principle, although the values are not exact. You can see there was a resistance level slightly above 11 in June and July, followed by a breakout on August 28. The new support level of 11.5 is just above the previous resistance.

There is an explanation for this in terms of the psychology of the market. Traders who did not buy while the stock was in the lower range may be regretting missing the opportunity. When the price comes down close to the range again, a number of them will be determined not to miss out again and decide to buy, which pushes up the demand and establishes the new support level.

The next step in discussing trading principles is the trend line. Remember, stock prices do not trend all the time, and when they are bouncing between the support and resistance lines, they are going sideways. But when a stock is in a trend, it is possible to draw a trendline that is sloping, and which represents an angled support or resistance line.

If a stock is in an uptrend, then the line will slope upward. You can draw it by connecting two or more low points on a price chart. It does not always work out, and there are some price charts with an upward trend that do not have a suitable position for a trendline. If you draw a trendline on the basis of two points, and a third low point touches it and bounces off, the trendline is considered confirmed and more reliable. As long as the stock price stays above the rising trendline, which is a support line, the trend is valid and can be traded on. If the price drops below, this is the same as a breakout downward and may signal the end of the trend.

If a stock is in a downtrend, the trend line will be drawn over the top of the prices and will represent a resistance line. Again, two points may be joined to start a trend line, but a third would give confirmation. Exactly where to draw a trendline, and how significant it is, are matters where the art aspect — rather than science — aspect of technical analysis comes in. There is no "true" answer, but the trendline can give you clues as to future price action.

Chart patterns

Another aspect of technical analysis is recognizing patterns in the pricing chart. This is even more of an art form, but with practice you will become familiar with several different price patterns that frequently can give a clue to the future price action you can expect. Patterns are used to give an early warning of a reversal of the trend, or sometimes to give a continuation signal, suggesting that the trend in place will be continuing.

One of the well-known patterns is called the head and shoulders pattern. This is because the chart forms three peaks with the middle one higher than the one on either side, suggesting the outline of a head and shoulders. This is a reversal pattern, which occurs in an uptrend, and suggests that the trend may be coming to an end. If you become attuned to spotting this pattern, you will find it is more often than not a sign that the bull run has finished, meaning that the rising pattern has finished, and the pattern will start falling in the opposite direction. The low points between the peaks are known as the neckline, and they suggest a support level. After the second shoulder, if the price drops below this support level, then the reversal is likely.

Another familiar pattern to technical analysts is the double top. This is another reversal pattern that occurs in an uptrend and is simpler than the head and shoulders, as it only requires two peaks. The trough between the peaks suggests a support level. The two peaks that fail to continue upward through resistance suggest that the uptrend is running out of steam, and you should look for the price to drop below the support to give an indication that the reversal has arrived.

Both the head and shoulders and the double-top patterns have an equivalent that can occur in a downward trend, suggesting a reversal to start an uptrend. The reverse head and shoulders pattern is the opposite of the head and shoulders, where the middle trough of the three will be the lowest point. The neckline — in this case, the two peaks between the troughs — will represent a resistance level, and reversal is confirmed when the price passes up through this point. The opposite of the double top is called a double bottom, with two troughs at a similar level. The peak between is the resistance level.

The patterns so far have been reversal patterns, signifying an end to the trend and the start of an opposite trend. The last pattern you should be familiar with that has a definite shape is called the cup and handle pattern, and it is a continuation pattern. This again occurs in an uptrend. The cup is formed when the price stops rising and goes down, only to rise back up to the same level again. This forms a bowl shape for the cup, and it is important that the shape is rounded and not a "V" for the pattern to be valid. The price goes on to dip again, though not as far down as the cup, before rising again to form the handle. The temporary resistance level is represented by the sides of the cup, so when the price has fallen to handle and breaks out above this level, the continuation of the uptrend is strongly indicated.

You will also see a family of patterns, called such things as wedges, triangles, and flags, which share a similar idea. For each of these you can draw a trendline connecting the high points, as well as a trendline connecting the low points, and the lines will converge. Effectively, you can think of the trend lines as squeezing the price range. When the range of prices has been squeezed enough, the price will break out of the triangle shape and start a new trend. These patterns are sometimes reversal patterns and sometimes continuation patterns, and it is often best to see in which direction the price breaks out before committing to a trade.

There are a number of other patterns that have been identified by the experts, but the ones covered in the previous sections are the ones you will most likely need to be familiar with when you invest in gold.

Candlestick charting

The essence of a candlestick chart was covered previously, but the power of them has not been revealed to you yet. They are considered to be an insight into the market, revealing the psychology of the traders who are influencing the prices. Because of their construction, it is easy to identify candlesticks and candlestick patterns that have significant meanings. For any investment, it is important to know some of the basic tenets and fundamental patterns candlestick charting shows.

First, candlesticks, or candles, come in various shapes and sizes, and these have significance. The white or black body of the candle may be short or long, and the lines that extend from the body up and down, sometimes called the wicks or shadows, will also vary in length; at times, they may be nonexistent if the open or close price is the same as the highest or lowest price.

In general terms, the longer the body, the stronger the market pressure is in the direction indicated by the body. A long white body indicates strong pressure for the price to go up. The bottom of the body was the opening price and the top is the closing price, so a big difference between them means the price has risen significantly over the day. The corollary is that a short body indicates no strong pressure and perhaps indecision in the market.

There is a special name for the candlestick that has a body with no length, which is where the opening and closing prices are the same. It is called a Doji, and it is considered of special significance, often signifying a reversal. There is also a special name for a candlestick that is all body, with no shadows at the ends, indicating that the price moved strongly from the opening value to the closing value without moving outside. This candlestick is called a Marubozu, and it counts as a strong indication that the trend is well-supported.

As mentioned, a Doji suggests that a reversal may be about to happen. In essence, the pattern means that the forces of supply and demand are in balance, with neither side dominating the price by the end of the day, so setting the scene for a reversal. However, a Doji is never a valid signal on its own; should be read in conjunction with the candlesticks that came before; and is more significant if the volume is substantial and if there are other technical indications that suggest a reversal may be due.

There are hundreds of identifiable candlestick patterns, involving up to four or five candles in different arrangements. Sometimes the patterns provide an indication that seems to be in conflict with what you might expect; for instance, a succession of strong moves in one direction may indicate a reversal, which the Japanese inventors of the method characterize as the market becoming "tired."

There are some basic principles that you must remember when you use candlestick charting to help in your trading:

- The candlestick shows the strength behind the price, as well as the price.

- A candlestick should never be considered alone, but always in the context of the market.

- If a candle signal is supported by another technical signal, then it is more likely to be successful.

- A candlestick does not indicate a price target.

Technical indicators

We now come to what is often referred to as the core of technical analysis: the technical indicators and oscillators. There are a number of these, and more are being invented all the time. They all result from calculations on historic data and present values or other indications to suggest future price movement. Many of them have parameters that can be selected by the user to adapt them to the particular security for better accuracy.

Some indicators can seem to perform with almost uncanny predictive powers, but the fact that there are many hundreds of indicators should alert you to the truth that there is no perfect indicator that does not fail. Regardless of the sophistication with which the indicator is designed, of necessity it can only be based on past performance and values, and cannot know what the future brings. Indicators only indicate, but they are useful to make sure that the odds are on your side when you make your trading selections.

The first indicator to be considered is the moving average. Most people know what an average is, and the simple moving average is an average of the price for the last X number of periods. This is sometimes shown as SMA (X), and calculated by adding together the recent prices and dividing by X. This indicator is actually a family of indicators with different values of X and different purposes in the technical analysis.

For example, SMA (200) is an average for the last 200 trading days, if using a daily chart, and may be used to provide a visual assessment of the long-term trend. SMA (50) provides a line that follows the prices more closely, and may serve as a support line. The actual number of periods to give the best support line is something that can be experimented with. In this case, if the price drops below the moving average, it indicates that the uptrend has ceased.

Taking a moving average for a shorter time, say ten days, you can have a simple buy/sell indicator. When the market price crosses the moving average line, you will buy or sell the stock, buying when the price goes above the average and selling when it drops below. This can work quite well on stocks that are well-behaved and exhibit clear trends, although there are times when it will be fooled by the market fluctuations. Again, you can experiment with the number of days to find the best-performing moving average. Another common method is to trade when the moving average line changes its direction, from going down to going up, for instance. This is called the level rule. It lags behind the signals given from the crossing, so it is slow in signaling the trade, but this can help eliminate excess trading.

A further development of this is to trade when two different moving averages cross each other — for example, when the SMA (5) crosses the SMA (20). This is really just a variation of the price crossing the moving average, as the price is effectively a one-day moving average. You can also get moving averages that weight the value toward the more recent price, and some traders prefer to use these. They are called exponential moving averages (EMA). The most important factor to remember when using moving averages for trading is that they are ineffective if the price is going sideways. They require a trending price so that they work. They are a lagging indicator, and they will seldom indicate the start of a trend. All they will do is alert you to a trend that has already started so that you can trade with it.

An extension to the idea of the moving average is captured in the indicator called Bollinger bands. This was invented by John Bollinger, and introduces the idea of volatility or the amount of fluctuation in a price to the moving average. It gives continually varying support and resistance levels. Bollinger bands include a moving average line for a settable number of time periods, often 15 or 20, and a line above or below, which is two standard deviations away from the moving average. Standard deviation is a statistical measure of volatility. The statisticians tell us that bracketing the moving average with the two standard deviation bands will include 95 percent of the typical price fluctuation.

Bollinger bands are useful in two ways. First of all, you will see that the price often follows the band: the upper band if it is a rising trend, and the lower band for a declining price. In a trending market, the price can seem glued to the band. If you are looking for a trade, you could do worse than buying the security when the price touches the upper band, and selling short if the price touches the lower band. Any time the price leaves the band and comes back toward moving average, it is an indication that the trend is losing steam, and it would be a good time to exit the position.

There is additional information from the distance between the upper and lower bands. If these move close together, squeezing into the price, then you should be on the lookout for a breakout, when the price will move rapidly up or down. The bands will give no indication which way is more likely, however.

There are many similar indicators that are drawn directly on the price chart, and give information or signals for trading. The final one mentioned here is the parabolic SAR, which was developed by Welles Wilder. SAR stands for stop and reverse. This indicator is often used to show where to put a stop-loss order. In effect, it creates a trailing stop on the chart. *See the later section on Placing Your Trade for a full explanation of the operation of the stop-loss and trailing stop.*

If the stock is in an uptrend, the parabolic SAR will be underneath the price movements, and you can adjust the stop-loss up to follow the line as the price increases. In a trending market, the SAR will indicate when to sell. If the uptrend hesitates, the SAR will jump to above the price, a clear indication that you should exit the trade. As with the previous indicators, it is a good idea to become familiar with this by experimenting on different charts and by putting different values into the formula.

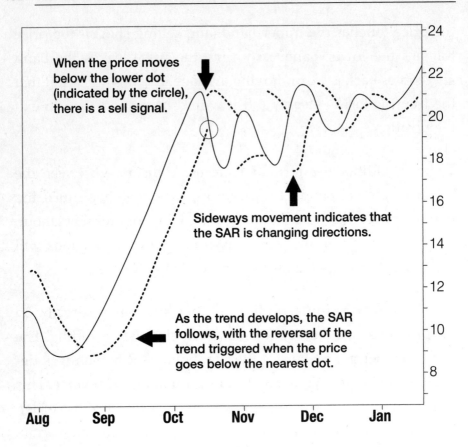

When the price moves below the lower dot (indicated by the circle), there is a sell signal.

Sideways movement indicates that the SAR is changing directions.

As the trend develops, the SAR follows, with the reversal of the trend triggered when the price goes below the nearest dot.

Many other indicators are usually shown graphically underneath the price chart. These can be divided into two groups: indicators that range around a center line, nominally zero, which help to indicate the direction of the price; and oscillators, which will go from one extreme to another, indicating an overbought or oversold condition when at the extreme.

A familiar indicator to many traders is the moving average convergence/divergence indicator (MACD). This was invented by Gerald Appel and is available on most charting packages. The purpose of this indicator is to try to overcome the problem mentioned with moving average crossovers — that of the indication lagging the price action. Appel tackled this by inventing an indicator that not only includes moving averages, but also considers the momentum with which these averages are approaching or going away from each other.

Before two moving average lines cross each other, they must converge together, and the MACD takes into account the speed with which they are approaching each other. If you were to plot the difference between two moving averages, then you would have a value of zero when they crossed, or converged, which is just a different way of viewing the same indication that moving averages can give to us. Appel's technique is to consider a moving average of the plot of the differences, and where this crosses the difference line provides an earlier indication of the trend change. Although you do not need to understand the mathematics of this, you should experiment and see for yourself the power of this concept.

Another way of looking at momentum is with the momentum indicator. Momentum is often calculated by a comparison of the current price with the price ten days ago. If there has been no change in price, the indicator will be zero. Following suit of basic mathematics, the indicator will be positive or negative according to the rate of change of price. The momentum indicator line may be rising or falling, or it may be horizontal. If it is horizontal, that does not mean the price is not changing, just that the price is changing at the same rate as it was ten days ago. Some people trade when the momentum indicator crosses the zero line, buying when the indicator crosses upward and going short when it goes downward. Others take a rising slope on the line to indicate that the trend is getting stronger and to confirm a long position.

The relative strength index (RSI) is another indicator that has its basis in momentum. It was conceived in order to give an early indication of a change in momentum. The momentum indicator may be delayed in crossing the zero line, giving a late signal. If, on the other hand, you take your signal as the change in direction of the momentum index, and you do not wait for it to cross zero, you risk the chance that the price move will not continue and will run out of steam. The RSI is designed to deal with this objection by considering the size of the average up move compared to the size of the average down move. The value of the RSI may be as much as 70 to 75 percent, when the stock will generally be considered overbought, and that is subject to too much buying enthusiasm and likely to reverse from its uptrend. The RSI may go down to 25 to 30 percent when it becomes a buying prospect, as it is oversold and too cheap. Any time that the RSI line is going in the opposite direction to the price line is a time to beware and look for the reversal in price.

An alternative indicator based on momentum is called the stochastic oscillator. This was invented by Dr. George Lane, and it enjoyed particular popularity amongst traders in the 1990s. It is unusual in that it considers more than just the closing price each day: It actually compares the stock's closing price to the whole range of prices that has been seen. When a stock is in an uptrend, it will tend to be toward the upper level of the range of prices, and the opposite for a down trend. The calculation is complex and can be reviewed in many trading books, but the result is an indicator that shows overbought above 80 percent, and oversold below 20 percent. The signal for trading is often taken as the move through the level — for example, if the indicator is below

20 percent, you would buy the security as soon as it passed up through that level.

There are many more indicators and oscillators available, but there are some important principles to keep in mind regardless of which index you use. There is no perfect indicator, and all indicators will be successful sometimes and fail other times. You do not have to review all indicators available, but it is a good idea to get confirmation of a likely trade by examining at least two pointers. In any case, you do not want to consider more than four or five indicators, as to do so would be counterproductive. It is best to select indicators that are based on different aspects of the price — for instance, a momentum-based indicator and a price-based indicator.

The secret of trading is not so much finding the correct security to buy, but the discipline to control your buying and selling, often known as money management. Whenever you enter a trade, you need to have two price values determined in advance. The first will be the price at which you get out of the trade if it does not go in the direction you expect. This is the amount you are risking. The second will be the price target if the security performs as you expect. This is the reward. You should not enter a trade unless the ratio of reward to the risk is three-to-one. Even if you only select half-correctly, you will still make a profit by sticking to this guideline.

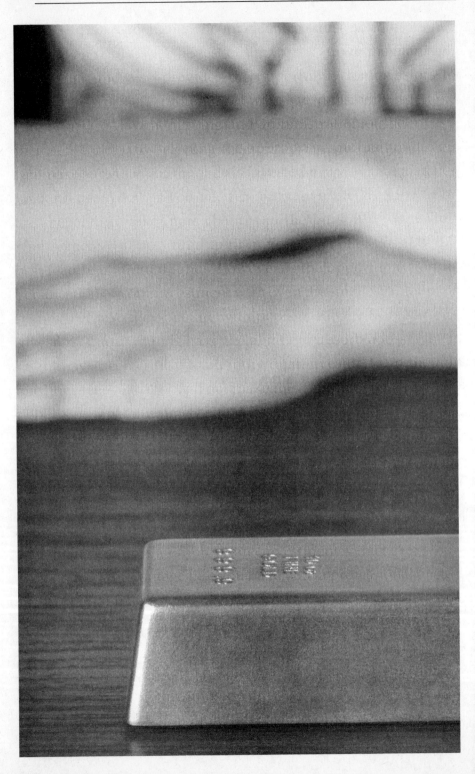

CHAPTER SEVEN

Finding a Broker

Whatever type of gold-related investing you plan to do, you will need to find a broker who can sell you the product you are after. Choice of a broker is one of the most important decisions you have to make because fees and commissions, and the amount of assistance you can expect, vary from company to company. Some brokers deal in more than one financial product, but if you want to invest in the whole range of gold-related financial instruments, you will probably need more than one broker.

In general, a broker acts as an agent for you when you are wanting to buy or sell stocks, bonds, and other commodities. The broker will thus facilitate your buying and selling of the product you want, and you can find companies that will recommend investments to you rather than leaving you to make your own selections. You can expect to pay higher fees if you require more service and attention from your broker.

When selecting a broker, you should look for the words "Member SIPC" in their signs and advertisements. SIPC, which stands for the Securities Investor Protection Corporation, is a nonprofit corporation funded by its members to protect investors' assets if their broker becomes bankrupt or financially troubled.

It is important to note that the SIPC does not protect against fraud, and it could not afford to compensate all victims of securities fraud. In this way, it is not the equivalent of the Federal Deposit Insurance Corporation (FDIC), with which you are probably familiar. The FDIC protects investors' money in banks. Congress realized when passing the act that formed the SIPC nearly 40 years ago that investors are prepared to take on a certain amount of risk in buying and selling securities. This is in contrast to investors who deposit money in banks, where there is a reasonable expectation that the money should be secure.

STOCKBROKERS

If the investments you are interested in are traded on the stock market, then naturally you will need to have an account with a stock brokerage. This would apply whether you are interested in long-term investments, or whether you would like to try trading for profit, taking shorter-term positions in equities. Whether you are conservative or aggressive, or seeking growth or value, a stock brokerage account will allow you to benefit from the numerous investments and strategies there are to choose from. If you already invest in the stock market, you may already have an account that you can use for your gold-related investments.

There are two basic types of stockbrokers: the full-service broker and the discount broker. Some brokerages combine elements of each, but for the sake of comparison, consider them as distinct types. The full-service broker may be the type you think of first when the word stockbroker is mentioned. This is the more traditional function, often portrayed in the movies, where the investor will engage in a dialogue with the broker who is offering recommendations for the investor's consideration. The full-service broker offers a myriad of services and a fee structure that reflects the time that the broker needs to keep up with the markets and prepare personal recommendations.

In contrast, the discount broker, which has become much more popular because of the Internet, starts on the basis of providing a trading place only, where a customer can give a specific direction to buy or sell and it will be implemented. The emphasis with a discount broker is on speedy and accurate execution at a minimal cost, as suggested by the name. Having said that, you will find that discount brokers have added an extensive range of facilities to their Web sites in the name of competition, and to attract the business away from other discount brokers. It would be unusual to find a broker who offers merely transactional privileges. You will usually find full charting facilities with access to many technical indicators; some methods for initial selection or sieving of the stocks; e-mail updates and e-mail alerts; and any other facilities that the broker can implement to help in your trading. Certainly, these facilities are merely a matter of programming and can be provided automatically without further time spent by the brokers' staff, but they do narrow the difference between full-service brokers and discount brokers.

OPENING AN ACCOUNT

It is a relatively simple matter to open an account at either type of broker. You can often complete most of the formalities online. If you want to trade "on margin," which is where the broker allows you credit to increase your effective trading capital, then there may be an additional check into your credit worthiness, and this is the broker protecting his or her interest and making sure as far as possible that as a client, you are going to be reliable. Most brokers allow you to open your account with very little capital, perhaps $1,000.

Even though it is an easy exercise to open an account, you should not rush into it. One of the first questions you should ask is the cost of commissions and any other fees that you may be expected to pay. Commissions, which are charged every time you trade, can vary from $7 with a discount broker, like Scottrade, to $24.95 or more at a more expensive broker. Some brokers additionally charge a percentage of the value, or on a cost per share. You will need to plan what quantity and what frequency you intend to trade to see how these costs may affect your portfolio.

You also need to do thorough research on the broker you are considering committing a substantial proportion of your portfolio to. There are some larger, well-known companies — such as Schwab and Scottrade, who have an established reputation — but you may also wish to consider a smaller company that can provide personal attention, particularly if you are looking for a full-service broker. The larger brokers often have local offices, where you can put a face to the name, and even if they are mainly online brokers, frequently you will be able to speak to local staff on the phone to sort out any problems.

If there is a choice of accounts that you can open at the broker you select, with various rates of commissions and trade expectations, you may find it helpful to talk with the local office and seek their advice. This will provide you with further assurance that the broker will be helpful when needed, and if this is not the case, it is not too late to decide to go elsewhere. If you foresee using options in your trading strategy, be sure to include that in your discussion so that the broker will set up your account correctly for this feature.

After you have completed the form, and the broker has done any checks that he or she requires — such as a bank reference — then you need to fund your account. Mailing or taking in a check will always be acceptable, but you may need to wait until it clears before the broker allows you to place trades. A frequently used alternative is a direct transfer from your bank account. Sometimes you can even arrange this with online banking, and transfer further investment capital manually or automatically on a schedule to your brokerage account.

Placing your trade

There are many different types of order you can use when placing trades, but they are fairly easy to understand, and you need to be familiar with them so that you can take full advantage of the different features. The simplest type of order is called a market order, and that just tells your broker to buy shares at the best price he or she can find right away. You should hear back within minutes that your order has been "filled," and you will be advised of the actual price and costs. With this method, you have no guarantee of the price you will pay, and it could be very different from the last price that you saw for the shares, particularly if the shares are thinly traded. You should also be aware that if you place a market order afterhours, this will be filled when the markets open on the next regular trading day. The opening price may be very different from the closing price on the previous day.

If you use an online broker, it is very easy to place an order from any computer with an Internet connection. The security of your account is safeguarded by having you log in with a password, and after that you can click through to your research and charts, select the stock, and place one of a variety of orders. Use the different types of orders that can be placed from a Scottrade account as examples of how this works.

Considering first the types of buy orders available, the next choice after a market order is a limit order. When using this, you enter a specific price (called a limit price, which is lower than the current price); this represents the most that you will pay for the stock. If the market reaches that price or lower, your broker will try to execute your order and buy the shares. So the limit order guarantees the price (or better) that you pay for the shares, but does not guarantee that the purchase is executed; the market order previously discussed guarantees that you buy the shares, but it does not guarantee what price you will pay.

Next in the list of orders with an online broker for Scottrade is the stop order, sometimes called the stop-loss order when used for selling shares. With a stop order you can enter a stop price, above the current price, and the trade will not be executed — the shares will not be bought — until the share price reaches it. Though you may think it sounds silly to wait for the price to go up before buying the shares, this type of order is useful if you think the price may "break out" from its pattern and take off. Placing this order costs you nothing and has no effect unless the share price does move up, in which case the order will be placed and you can benefit from the remainder of the move. With a stop order, it is important to note that there is no guaranteed price. When the share price reaches the stop price, this simply triggers a market order, which will buy the shares at the best price available.

The stop-limit order is a combination of the above orders. In this, you place a limit price and a stop price for your order, which has the effect of overcoming the limitations of the stop order noted in the last couple of sentences above. The stop-limit order controls your entry to the trade, waiting until the price starts taking off before authorizing the purchase, but once triggered, you will not pay more for the stock than your limit price. Obviously, this has the risk that your order may not be filled if the price is going up rapidly, which would perhaps be a shame, but you have the choice and can control your risk.

You may not find the "trailing buy" stop order used much — a trailing stop is more commonly used in selling to minimize losses and get out of a trade when it turns against you, as you will see in the description below. But the effect of the trailing buy is to set a movable stop-order price that will go down if the share price drops before the order is triggered. The movable price will not go up when the stock price rises, and when it is hit, the order becomes a market order to buy. You can select for the stop price to be a certain percent or a certain number of points away from the market price.

The final choice for a buying order is a "buy to cover" order. Buying to cover is the term used when you close out a short position — you are buying shares to cover the shares that you borrowed to take the short position. A full explanation of "going short" is in the previous trading section. Remember, going short means that you buy the stock when it is high, with a plan of selling it when it is lower. You can combine a buy to cover order with some other order variations, such as the trailing stop. This would allow the stock price to go down further, increasing your profit, before rising to hit the stop price and close out the trade.

On the selling side, the simplest is again the market order, where you receive whatever price the market is prepared to pay the second you place your order for your shares. There is no guarantee of the price, but if you see the share price falling, you may decide to sell as quickly as you can, and this would be an appropriate order to achieve that. As with buying, the market order guarantees that the transaction will proceed, but it cannot guarantee the price.

You can use a limit order when you are selling, and for this you will put in a limit price — the price, or higher, at which you are prepared to sell your shares. If the price reaches this level for long enough for the broker to execute the trade, then you will have sold the shares; otherwise, there is no guarantee of execution. In a similar way to the buying example, the market order guarantees execution without guaranteeing price; the limit order guarantees price without guaranteeing execution.

When you are selling shares, the sell-stop order requires you to enter a stop price, which is below the current market price. This is done to prevent further losses, or to protect a profit from stock prices that may continue to drop. If the share price falls until it hits this level, then the order is triggered and becomes a market order. This means that the broker will sell your shares at the best price he or she can; it may not be as much as the stop price you requested, but it should be close. As mentioned before, the sell-stop order is often used to protect profits in a winning trade by forcing the shares to be sold before the price falls back to your original entry price, thus allowing you to make money on the investment. Traders talk of "adjusting their stops," and this usually means adjusting the stop price of their sell-stop orders closer to the market price after the shares have increased in value. If no adjustments are made and a share increases in value, then there will be a big margin between the stop price and the value of the shares, meaning that the shares are ultimately less profitable for the investor. Thus, adjustment is necessary.

The trailing stop order is usually used when selling, not buying, shares, as mentioned earlier. The idea of this is that the price of a stop order "trails" the market price, staying a fixed distance away while the price is rising, but never going back down. Eventually, when the price of the share comes down to meet the value of the trailing stop order, the shares are sold automatically, preserving most of the profit. The distance that the price of the stop order is from the market price can be set to be a percentage of the price or an actual value.

Finally, the last type of sell order is to sell short. As explained in the trading section, this involves selling shares when you are short of them, i.e., you do not have any of the shares. If the price of the shares goes down as you expect, you then buy to cover and profit from the fact that you paid less for the shares that they were worth when you started the trade. Although it sounds confusing, the details are taken care of by your broker, and all you have to do is think of this as a straightforward way of profiting from a value going down.

Some of these orders can have modifiers applied or added to them. One of these is called AON, which stands for "all or nothing." It is an instruction to the broker that you want the exact number of shares you have requested in the order, and if the total amount cannot be bought then you want nothing. It cannot be used with the market order, where the broker will buy the requested shares as quickly as he reasonably can, which may mean that he buys them in several lots to make up the numbers. It can be applied to a limit order, and in this case the order will only be executed if all the shares requested can be bought in a single lot at the limit price. This imposes an additional restriction on executing the order and may make it less likely to be fulfilled. AON cannot be applied to any other types of orders, like market orders.

An important part of every order that you place — except the market order, which is fulfilled as quickly as possible — is the duration for which you want the broker to keep trying to execute the order. For instance, you may specify that the order must be completed "today," and this is called a day order. If the conditions for the order to be placed have not occurred by the end of the trading day, then the day order will expire and never be executed. For instance, the price may not reach your limit price, so the order would not be triggered. Usually if you place a day order online after the market closes, it is taken to be intended for the next working day and would expire after that if not fulfilled. Because the trading is limited to the time period of one day, investors who utilize day trading have the chance to substantially increase their earnings. This is true for any market type, as day traders can take long or short positions, based on the day's stock market trends. Plus, news or events of the next day will not affect the shares of the day traders, as it would if another type of trading was used.

Another way that an order can be specified is as "good until canceled" (GTC). The order will remain active until it is filled, until you cancel it, or until some arbitrary date a month or two in the future, depending on the broker. If you fully intend to go through with the trade, this is the type of order that you will be using. You must be careful to keep a note of the orders that you have open so that you do not over-commit your funds and suddenly find the broker trying to complete several different orders.

The other common choice for the duration of an order is "good 'til date" (GTD). This simply means that the broker will keep trying to execute the trade until the date that you set.

Setting your duration is not only important when you initially place an order, but it is also important to keep in mind while your broker is working for you. By keeping the lines of communication open with your broker, you will be able to keep track of the durations you set for each option and whether they have been met.

The Internet advantage

The Internet has made it much easier to stay in touch with your broker and for your broker to let you know when anything important happens in the markets. You can choose to be notified when a share price reaches a certain level, and you can receive nightly updates of how your shares are doing. It is possible to setup automatic triggers that will initiate a communication from your broker, alerting you to price changes that you may be interested in.

These facilities are available from many brokers, even the discount ones, and may influence your decision when you are checking out which broker to use. You should find that the broker will allow you to log in and "play" with the company's Web site to see if you find the controls and displays available to your liking. The Internet even allows you to have streaming displays, giving you the same information as professional traders have. This usually involves some additional software from your broker and a monthly charge, and is not necessary for most trading activity.

Account margins

Your brokerage account may be set up to give you a margin for trading. Usually, the broker will lend you as much money as you have in your account, doubling your ability to buy stocks and shares. When you are starting out, it is not advisable to take advantage of this facility, as it will allow you to lose money more quickly while you are learning.

Keep in mind that when your broker is lending you money, it is not free. You will be charged interest on the margin that you use, so the more you borrow, the more you will have to pay. Once you are confident of your trading ability, you will learn to appreciate the facility, but up until that time, it may be wise for you to ignore the existence of the margin so you do not increase your chances of losing money.

GOLD BROKER

If you are interested in dealing with the physical metal, in the form of bullion bars, bullion coins, or numismatics, then you will need to find another type of broker, as a stockbroker will not handle these items. A gold broker can give you professional advice about buying and selling gold, and you can find many by doing an online search. Once again, you need to exercise care in reviewing the broker to use. A flashy Web site is no indication of a sound company, and you should check for references, as well as with the Better Business Bureau (BBB) to make sure that the company is soundly based and has not been the subject of complaints.

If you choose to use an online broker, you will find that competition requires them to charge reasonable rates when selling gold. In truth, there are not many gold brokers on the high street, so you may have little choice in the type of broker that you use. If you are selling gold, you have the option of visiting a pawn shop, but that is unlikely to be the best place to maximize the return on your investment.

When you sell to an online gold broker, you will usually receive an insured mailer in which to send the goods. It is worth checking on the insurance to make sure that you are 100 percent covered, and be sure to read the fine print. After the broker receives your mailer, you will be contacted with an offer, and you can then decide whether to take it. Be sure you have undertaken research into your items and have an understanding of their true worth. If they are bullion items, they can be valued by taking into account their weight and the current gold pricing, and reducing this value by a small profit margin for the broker. You may have more difficulty in being offered an acceptable value for any numismatic coins, as the premium involved with these will be up to the dealer's judgment.

Should you decide that you do not want to accept the broker's offer, your goods should be returned to you promptly and fully insured. If you do sell, then you should expect prompt payment from a reputable company.

COMMODITY BROKERS

Since 1971, when President Richard Nixon closed the gold window, gold has traded as a commodity and has not been considered a currency. What better place then to buy your gold than at a commodity broker? If you want to trade commodities, which basically means to invest in the futures markets, you will need a futures brokerage account. You can find out some information on futures brokers from the U.S. Commodity Futures Trading Commission (CFTC) at **www.cftc.gov**, which ensures that the market users and the public are protected from fraud when it comes to traded commodities. You can also find information about opening a futures brokerage account at the Chicago Mercantile Exchange (CME) Web site, **www.cmegroup.org**, an organization that aims to reduce the risk for customers who invest in futures or options.

Being a commodity broker is much more specialized than a stockbroker, and although you might find many friends who use a stockbroker and know something about their function, there will be few who trade commodities. As with most professions, the commodity broker needs to be licensed and registered, and that is done by the National Futures Association (NFA), **www. nfa.futures.org**. The broker will take what is called a Series 3 examination, which is all about futures markets and contracts, and will be designated an associated person. The company they work for will be registered under one of a variety of names, such as introducing broker (IB), or futures commission merchant (FCM).

As with choosing a stockbroker, you should take care to check into the company's record, examining professional registrations and Better Business Bureau information. Trading futures is a risky enough business without wondering if your broker is not going to perform, or even going to defraud you. Because of the inherent risk with futures trading, you will find that you have to sign a number of agreements, verifying that you acknowledge the risk of loss. The broker will want to know your income, value, and the extent of your trading experience, and will evaluate how much of a margin can be extended to you. As pointed out before, the broker routinely lends you money for this form of trading, so you should expect to be checked for your creditworthiness and ability to pay.

BEWARE OF SCAMS AND PITFALLS

Where appropriate in the preceding text, mention has been made of various scams that have been tried, and in the realm of gold investing, because of the high value, it seems there are many people trying to commit fraud. It is worth going through the various ways in which you could be exposed to trickery so that you will not become a victim.

Particularly in times when investing in gold and other precious metals is becoming fashionable and obvious to the general public, scam artists will come out of the woodwork and try to take advantage of the many people who are ignorant of the real workings of the markets. One trait that many of them share in common is that they are skilled at sounding legitimate, and can usually answer any of the questions that come to mind. It is important that you know the reputation of the firm that you are dealing with, and that you initiate the telephone call rather than accepting that a caller is bona fide and represents the company he or she says.

If you are in the market for buying gold, then you may come across a storage scam. This is where the seller will sell you the metal and then contract with you to provide secure storage for it, citing problems you may have with security and your insurance if you take delivery. It has been known for even major firms to have defaulted in this respect, telling their customers that the gold is secure, but secretly taking a chance that not all the customers will request delivery at the same time, and not holding the total amount of gold that has been purchased. In some cases, this may even start as the company gambling on the market, thinking that the price of gold will go down, and they will buy the required quantity at a lower rate before you have missed it. In other cases, it is more straightforward, and the deceit is intended from the outset.

The one sure way to avoid this scam is to never store your metals with the seller. You might make an exception if the seller was an extremely well-established company, properly insured and regulated, and preferably with a trust fund and independent trustee to look after your interests. Even then, it would be a good idea to look at the gold and make sure that your name is attached to it. The only advantage in leaving your gold bullion stored with the seller, apart from having to find somewhere else to store it, is that you will not have to resubmit for an assay when you sell the gold, ultimately saving you time and money. You might also consider buying bullion coins instead, as they will have a determined value and can be stored at home.

Particularly when it seems that gold is increasing in value reliably, you may come across another scam perpetrated by the gold sellers. It may not be a fully fledged scam in the sense that it is an outright fraud, but it is certainly a situation that may turn against you, and about which you may not be adequately warned by the vendor. In this version, the gold salesperson is quite often on commission, and his or her goal is to encourage you to buy more gold than you have money for. There is a way to do this, and it is called buying "on margin," which is the same thing as borrowing money from the broker or dealer to buy an additional quantity. In essence, the gold seller is not scamming you with making false promises or selling a faulty product, but is instead scamming you by trying to pressure you into buying large quantities of gold, even if you do not have the money for it at the time of the purchase.

For stocks, quite often a broker will offer you 50 percent margin, which means you would only have to have half the money in your account for the purchase you want to make. You will find that the margin requested when buying gold may be as little as 10 percent, which means you can buy ten times as much gold as the amount of money you have at present.

An example of this sort of transaction that will be more familiar to you would be buying a house. You put a little down, say 10 percent, and the mortgage company will lend you the remainder of the money for your purchase. The case of buying a house is much more borrower-friendly, as mortgage rates are competitively bid and set, and may be half the rate charged by the gold dealer. You can also qualify for tax relief on the interest paid to buy a house. The only way in which buying gold on margin can be better than buying a house is if gold steadily increases in value; then, you would not need to make any regular payments because the value of your account is increasing, and that covers the interest charges. On the other hand, if the value of gold starts to decrease, so does your account, which means that you are not making enough money to cover the interest and the extra percentage of funds that you still need to pay from your initial purchase of the gold.

The salesman will explain the apparent advantages of buying on margin, and on the face of it you are able to make a much greater profit with your money by taking part in this transaction. If you buy ten times as much gold as the amount of money you have, and gold rises in value by 10 percent, then in theory you have doubled your money. For instance, with $1,000, you could buy $10,000 worth of gold. With a 10 percent rise in value, this would be worth $11,000, so you have gained as much as the money you invested: $1,000.

What will not be so obvious, however, is that you will pay what may be an exorbitant rate of interest for the money you borrow from the dealer. If gold takes several months to increase in value, you will find that the interest mounts up, eating into any possible profits. Secondly, the leverage in this transaction will work both ways. If the same $10,000 worth of gold lost 10 percent and fell to $9,000, you would have completely lost your original investment, as well as owed the dealer interest. In practice, you would hear from the dealer before this situation arose, as he or she would give you a "margin call," asking you to send more money to cover losses to date, or he would liquidate your position. You can compare this with the early 2009 real estate situation of the house prices dropping, and the number of houses that went into foreclosure when the owners owed more than the house was worth.

If you spend any time studying the charts of commodity prices, you will know that even if a market is bullish, the price will fluctuate up and down during its rise, so the possibility of a margin call is not unlikely. You need to be very careful before you enter into one of these contracts, and they are only really suitable for people who like to gamble and are aware of the risks they are taking. You will also find that you pay much higher commission charges for actually purchasing the metal if you buy ten times as much, and you should not expect the basic commission rate to be low if you are dealing with a company that encourages this kind of reckless investment.

Another trading method that you may come across involves "certificates" and "pool accounts." These are really promises that may be only worth the paper they are printed on, but they may be sold to you on the basis that they are cheap. The attraction is that such "purchases" appear very easy to do. Above all, you should not be fooled into thinking that these deals involve actually buying gold or other precious metals — all you are really getting is a promise to supply gold one day. Look at it this way: If the company is not charging you storage fees, this may not be a good thing, as it shows that there is nothing at present to store.

In fact, if you ever wanted to take delivery of the gold that the certificates are supposed to represent, you are likely to be charged an additional fee, sometimes called a "fabrication charge," which provides further evidence that the gold does not exist in your name until that time. Many of the companies running these schemes are using them to "short" the metal. They take your money and give you a promise, but do not go out and buy the metal for you. It is similar to selling gold short, which is a trading technique normally used to make money in a falling market by selling shares of gold that you do not actually own. You do this in the hopes that the price will fall and you can buy it back cheaper later, pocketing the difference between the selling price and the buying price. If the price rises, then the company will have to find the difference between what you paid and how much the gold costs. Some companies will use new investor cash to make up the difference, and this is obviously unsustainable.

If you are attracted to numismatic investments, you will have to be prepared for gold to go up a great deal in value, or for some particular circumstance to make your collection of coins more desirable before you can hope to see a profit. Remember that for most coins in ordinary collections, the value varies significantly with public sentiment, and seldom seems to move in your favor. If you try to sell back to the dealer where you bought them, you may be very disappointed at the offer you receive. In this respect, you should note that bullion coins are a much safer investment, tracking closely to the gold value, so if you are not particularly interested in coin collecting, numismatics are probably not for you.

If you do decide to invest in numismatics, however, then you should be careful to make sure that what you are buying is the genuine article. Most counterfeit coins are counterfeit numismatics, for the simple reason that counterfeiting bullion coins is much less profitable. Numismatics can be made from the correct type and weight of metal, as so much of the value is in the form of the coin and not the weight. It is comparatively simple to duplicate a design and make a reproduction.

It may not even be necessary for the fraudster to arrange for a reproduction to be made. A great many counterfeit coins start out as replicas of the originals, which is quite legal to mint and sell at a reasonable price. At some stage in their lives, the owner of these coins decides to pass them off as authentic, and thus they move into the realm of counterfeits.

You are not necessarily guaranteed the genuine article if you buy certified coins, as there are ways that this can be faked. For instance, a scammer can submit genuine coins to a grading service and obtain certification; once returned, there are ways in which the coins can be substituted with lesser quality or counterfeit devices, even though they are sealed in an apparently tamper-proof container. It is also possible for a scammer to buy the tamper-proof slabs direct from the manufacturer, and then this is a simple matter of forgery of a certificate to make "certified-graded" coins out of counterfeits or inferior examples.

If you have ever been attracted to television and magazine advertisements for selling your precious metals, then you may need to think again. You are unlikely to get the best deals by responding to these advertisements, and there are a couple of reasons why it is easy to see that you cannot hope for a fair price. First of all, TV and magazine advertising is expensive, which means that the dealer will have to mark up the sales price to be sure to cover the costs. Secondly, the lead time, particularly for monthly magazines, will be at least a couple of months, and the dealer is going to want to anticipate price fluctuations so that he or she does not end up out-of-pocket. Again, the printed price should be expected to be higher than it needs to be in order for the dealer to cover costs.

There is another way in which a dealer who chooses to advertise in this manner can cover costs. If there is a "too good to be true" offer, then you should expect to suffer a barrage of upsell rhetoric when you call the 1-800 number. Sometimes the offer will be in the form of a club with a monthly subscription and automatic shipment until canceled. While it may sound attractive over the phone, you would be wise to do your homework and discover the real market value of the items on offer.

When you are dealing with items such as gold, with a high value, it is always wise to go to a reputable dealer to take as much care as possible that you are buying the genuine article. There are ways that you can buy gold over the Internet that are fairly secure, but there are also many scams associated with this format. It is important to be able to verify that you are buying from a reputable source, and the appearance of a Web site or seals of approval and letters of commendation is no guarantee that the company is genuine. Some things to look for when it comes to the reputation of a gold dealer are:

- the dealer's length of service
- the amount of gold the dealer has access to
- testimonials from other customers

If you still feel driven to buy over the Internet from an auction site, such as eBay®, then the least you should do is pay using Pay-Pal, with a credit card to supply the funds to PayPal. This does not guarantee that you will be able to get your money back if something goes wrong with the transaction, but it does give you some of the best protection that you can get if the goods do not turn up or are not as described.

On the other hand, if you are selling goods on eBay, you may want to avoid offering PayPal. It is not unknown, particularly with buyers from other countries, for the buyer to claim that the article never arrived and to receive a refund some weeks later from PayPal, which is then deducted from your account. To safeguard yourself, you should always purchase insurance on goods that you send, and you can do this at the buyer's expense if you include that in your auction, or your agreement. Anything valuable should be sent with a traceable delivery, as this provides further evidence, even though it is possible for the buyer to claim that they received a parcel but the contents were missing or not as described.

To be clear, these scams can be perpetrated on many different Internet auction and selling sites. The previous example is given to detail the types of scams that you have to watch out for when you buy and sell over the Internet. Remember that these scams come in all different forms and from all different types of people, and do not just exist in the virtual world. Your best bet when investing in gold or other precious metals is to exercise caution; do your research and make sure the broker or dealer you are preparing to work with is reputable and certified.

CHAPTER EIGHT

The Other One

Although the focus of this book is the value of gold and how to profit from it, it will not have escaped your attention that there has been an increasing interest in the silver market, too, with some investment experts claiming that it is set to perform many times better than gold. Certainly, the odd commentator can be found who says that silver is merely riding on the coattails of gold, but there is a weight of expert opinion that says that silver has some catching up to do, and has been overlooked and forgotten in the shadow of gold.

That said, the silver market is volatile, which means you must be prepared for a roller coaster ride when you follow the price. There are more than enough positive reasons to include silver in your portfolio. Supply and demand indicates that silver will perform well in the future, although the reason why — because the supply is dwindling or because the demand is growing with new uses being discovered regularly — is a matter of debate.

Because silver is the metal that boasts the most industrial uses, and more are added to the list all the time, it can be fascinating to look at the applications that it is used for. For a variety of industrial uses, there is no substitute for silver. Silver is used to make batteries, both disposable and rechargeable. These batteries are used in watches, tools, and many other electronic devices.

Silver is highly conductive and frequently used for plug-in connectors on electronic devices, such as computers. It is also used for the wafer on–off switch. A number of chemical reactions used in manufacturing depend on silver to act as a catalyst; for example, it is a critical component in the production of plastics. Paper, dinnerware, buttons, handles, packaging materials, and insulation materials cannot be manufactured without using silver, and it is also needed for production of molded products.

Steel bearings are sometimes electroplated with silver because it aids in the joining of material, and electroplated silver cups and trophies are common. Tradesmen who work with piping, such as those in the air-conditioning, refrigeration, automobile, and airplane industries, will be familiar with silver, as joints are made using silver-brazing alloys.

Finally, silver is a bactericide and algaecide, and it has a number of pharmaceutical and medical applications. More ways of using it are being discovered all the time.

Why Buy Silver?

For all the reasons that you may be looking at buying gold, there are parallel reasons in the silver story. As discussed, the many

uses of silver are being expanded, and it offers wonderful investment opportunities and technological uses. Silver has proved
essential in photography and is integral to electronics, solar energy, and as a bactericide. Because of its qualities, it can be used
to make mirrors, and as technology advances, silver is finding a
market in many more areas.

Silver is not regarded in the same way as gold, which has always
been the ultimate status symbol. But there are several reasons
why it may prove to be a more profitable investment than gold
over the next few years. There certainly seems to be agreement
that it is currently in a bull market, meaning it has great potential
to move upward, just as gold is on the rise. Because of the rising
demand, coupled with the dwindling supply, silver seems sure to
outperform gold.

One of the reasons cited for silver to perform better than gold
has to do with supply and demand. The supply of silver will not
meet the growing demand for it, particularly as it is often produced as a by-product of other metal extraction. For example, a
mine producing base metal may find some silver content in the
ore, which will be separately extracted and sold on the market.
It is believed that most of the silver that is easily accessible has
already been mined, so future supply of new silver will be much
more difficult, even for mines that are specifically geared toward
producing silver. Most of the silver in the world is in India in
the form of jewelry. Understandably, there is little inclination for
the owners of heirloom silver jewelry to submit their pieces for
melting down, so much of this is not available for other uses. The
combination of silver becoming harder to mine, and being under private ownership that does not readily turn over the supply,

means that new industrial uses will add to silver's scarcity in the future. By contrast, gold is still being mined, and as the metal is a long-time symbol of status, it has been readily traded. Also, most of the world's gold does not exist in the form of jewelry, which facilitates trading and investment.

There are a number of factors that are currently contributing to silver's promising performance. First of all, silver is no longer as plentiful as it was. In 2003, the government stockpile dwindled completely, and the U.S. was already using more silver than can be produced. Already, in the years when silver is in high demand, there is a shortfall of some 200 million ounces, and new uses for silver are coming up frequently. China, India, and other parts of the world will continue to drive the demand for silver upward, and it is easy to see that the coming years will be marked by an incredible silver deficit.

Another advantage of silver over gold is that silver is inherently more affordable. This, combined with the factors previously mentioned, translates into the fact that silver is becoming rarer than gold. This is not to suggest that silver will reach the heights of gold's value, as there is more to the price and value than the amount of supply, but this is a powerful pressure for silver's price to increase more rapidly. The demand for silver, because of its monetary and industrial uses, is growing at a rate that mining cannot possibly keep up with. In past years, silver-producing mines have found veins of the metal that were fairly easy to tap into. Many of these veins have now been largely used up, making it increasingly difficult to mine and extract silver.

While silver is affordable for the average investor, it is rare enough to be prized. The world supply of silver is less than one-third of the supply of gold. At one time there was more than enough silver to go around, but it has been many years since production has been able to meet the demand for silver. In the case of silver that is mined as a by-product of other mining, there is little incentive to increase the production rate, as it will not help the overall profitability of the mine to any great extent.

CASE STUDY: DAVID MORGAN

David Morgan - Founder
www.silver-investor.com
support@silver-investor.com
(509) 464-1651

My interest in the precious metals began as an 11-year-old boy. I had been receiving an allowance of one silver quarter per week, and during that year, 1965, the coin went from 90 percent silver to a copper coin plated with zinc. Intuitively, I sensed that the two coins could not be of equal value, even though the political commentary at the time pretended they were. This began my lifelong quest into the study of money, metals, and mining.

Although I am very familiar with gold, my primary focus is on the silver market. In order to make a substantial amount of money investing, people need to define major trends and invest accordingly. I called the top in the stock market (2000) and the bottom in the commodity sector. I urged people to shift from paper (stocks) into things (commodities). The precious metals happen to be the top tier of all the commodities because they have remained free from default for over 5,000 years.

My philosophy is to buy real metal (coins or bars) and then branch out into top-tier, cash-rich, unhedged mining companies. After that, people can invest in more speculative areas, such as exploration companies. My greatest success has been calling the all-time bottom in the silver market and, from that time until now, providing information to people all over the world to help them understand the benefits of an honest money system.

I have learned that in order to be of maximum service to my readers, I must continue to learn. I am an avid reader of material dealing with economics, monetary history, geopolitics, and, of course, the precious metals. The biggest surprise about investing in precious metals is how few people understand the way the world's monetary system actually works. I see a huge rush into gold and silver over the next several years as more and more people strive to profit from this arena.

I recommend that new investors get educated before investing any actual money into the sector. My Web site provides a free newsletter with the Ten Rules of Silver Investing that provides a great deal of useful information to investors. This sector is one of the most exciting and volatile in existence, so be warned it is not for everybody. However, for those who can hold on to the bull, the rewards will be exceptional.

Contact:

www.Silver-Investor.com
www.TheMorganReport.com
www.gettheskinnyonsilver.com
support@silver-investor.com

SILVER MINING & EXTRACTION

Unlike gold, much of the silver in the world is in shallow deposits. Also unlike gold, much of the silver in the world is only extracted as a by-product of mining for another metal. The story of silver mining is very different to the gold story, even though the metals are bound up with each other in their usage as conveyors of wealth and currency.

Silver was first mined in Europe and West Asia. It was fairly easy to find and helped pay for Athens' development and expansion, as already mentioned in the gold section. But there is evidence that it had been mined much earlier than that in Turkey, which was then called Anatolia — the first major source of silver to the Asian continent. The deposits being mined as early as 4000 BC. were mixed with lead, and silver had to be extracted from the lead ore.

However, it was undoubtedly the silver mines of Laurium, near Athens, that were the first major producers, and it is estimated that production was as high as 1 million to 1 ½ million ounces a year at its peak. This production rate was the highest of any mine for centuries, and Laurium was still considered the largest individual mine up to the first century AD.

In time, mining in Spain became the dominant source of silver and remained so for 1,000 years. Spanish silver was supplied to the Roman civilization and used for bartering for spices on the Asian trade routes. Spanish silver was supplemented with silver mined in Greece, Asia Minor, and Italy, later joined by Germany and Eastern Europe, but it is doubtful whether the supply from all these sources ever exceeded the amount extracted in Laurium. After the Roman conquest, Roman Britain was also a source of lead ore from which silver was extracted.

The process by which silver was separated from lead included smelting, and it is thought that many miners died of lead poisoning. Because of this threat, sometimes slaves were forced to work in the mines.

From the mid-fifteenth century, silver began to be extracted from copper ores found in Germany, when Georg Agricola is credited with finding a method called liquation to separate the two metals. This method still involved smelting and lead, with the ore being heated to a temperature that would melt lead but not the copper. The molten lead-silver mixture was drained away for further processing. This basic method continued to be used until the nineteenth century.

In fact, there is evidence that the liquation process had been used in previous centuries, but it was widely adopted following Agricola's "discovery," and it is thought that production of silver increased as much as five times as a result. The process had a major impact on many industries — for instance, the copper produced through liquation helped in expanding the brass-making industry. Even the production of lead had to be stepped up, as so much was required for the liquation process.

With the discovery of the New World in 1492, there were further increases in silver production. In Bolivia alone, about 1 billion ounces of silver were produced in the seventeenth and eighteenth centuries, and Mexican mines had an output of 1.5 billion ounces in just one century. Peru produced 3 billion ounces from 1600 to 1800. These three countries accounted for about 85 percent of world silver production in this period.

Even though the gold rush is the best-known precious metal happening in the U.S., the silver rush was also a big event, with silver being found in Colorado and Nevada. The first major deposit found was the Comstock Lode in Nevada in 1859. The town of Leadville, Colorado, which is at more than 11,000 feet, was another significant source.

During the last two decades of the twentieth century, following the irrational exuberance that had pushed gold to record highs in 1980, mining for precious metals scaled down, which is one reason that it is not likely that production can be ramped up quickly in the near term. Most of the easily mined silver has already been dug up, and reserves are not great. Silver production was not abandoned, as silver benefits from the fact that it is a by-product of mining other metals. For instance, while copper is needed, silver will also be produced.

What has helped in recent history is that techniques to separate silver from other material have improved dramatically. This has been necessary as the quality of the ore has deteriorated, with all the better resources having been consumed already.

These techniques include froth flotation, patented in 1869 by William Haynes, and rediscovered at the beginning of the twentieth century by Charles Potter, a brewer, and Guillaume Delprat, a Spanish immigrant to Australia. This is perhaps the most widely used process for mineral extraction. It separates and concentrates mineral particles by using a froth. The ore is ground into a fine powder and mixed with water that contains chemicals which control how wetted the particles can become. When the water is aerated by blowing bubbles through it, wetted particles remain in the solution, and the dust that is unwetted floats on top of the bubbles. This process can be used on inferior ores to make the recovery possible when it could not be achieved with other methods.

Another improved technique, called electrolytic refining or electro-refining, was discovered by Dr. Emil Wohlwill. His initial process was based on separating gold and silver by using an impressed electric current. You can compare this process to that which is used to chromium plate parts of cars. By making the electric current flow from an anode to a cathode, you can make the metal in solution deposit on the cathode. This is called electrodeposition, and because it works on atomic basis, it results in very pure metal.

REVIEWING THE PAST

Silver has been mined since around 3000 BC. It was reasonably plentiful and easy to mold into jewelry and containers. In the early days of silver, it was used alongside gold as a currency, and as it has a lesser value, it was used for smaller purchases. Like gold, silver has been a popular form of currency since the ancient times. Both gold and silver have exhibited intrinsic value, and for centuries, the ratio between the two metals has determined that about 12 ounces of silver is equivalent to 1 ounce of gold. This has varied depending on the region of the world and the era, and is just an average. In China, it reached 4 ounces of silver to 1 ounce of gold, and back in ancient Egypt, the two metals were about on par.

You may wonder why there was this variation, but the answer is that there is no reason for gold and silver to be in any particular ratio. It is a result of market forces, and the value is found by an economic principle called "price discovery." Price discovery in its simplest form involves buyers and sellers settling on a price based on supply and demand. This is self-regulating, in that if the amount of goods for sale decreases, and the demand remains the same or increases, the price will typically increase until there is a balance re-established.

In fact, this process starts with something called "price determination," and price discovery includes other market factors. Price determination is simply the price suggested by the supply and demand curves, determined by looking at where they intersect. Price discovery involves other concepts, such as the market structure, size and competitiveness of the market, information available to the traders, and so on. In this case, as gold and silver are similar in many ways, it is likely that the average price ratio of 12 to 1 is simply a reflection of the ratio of the quantities of the metals in circulation, in other words there has probably been about 12 times as much silver as gold available, and ancient records would seem to bear this out.

Toward the end of the nineteenth century, more silver was discovered, and supplies increased significantly. The value of silver relative to gold went down until it reached a point where 1 ounce of gold could buy about 100 ounces of silver. Then government stepped in to change the dynamics of the system. President Franklin Roosevelt signed an act called the Silver Purchase Act of 1934, and the effect was that the U.S. Treasury began to amass a great stock pile of silver.

The Silver Purchase Act was a way of addressing one of the problems of the Great Depression. Many people were pressing Congress to give subsidies to silver miners, in view of the way the price had sunk so low. In response, the Silver Purchase Act nationalized domestic stocks of silver and required the Treasury to purchase silver until the price reached $1.29 per ounce, or until the value of the silver held was as much as a third of the value of the government's gold holdings. You will recall that at the same time, gold was being confiscated and revalued to $35 per ounce.

The Silver Purchase Act had many consequences, some of which were not intended. It drove the silver market offshore and virtually ruined the New York silver market. The U.S. Treasury even bought 60 million ounces of silver from London, which served to benefit foreign speculators. The total cost of the exercise was said to have been $1.5 billion, which in those times was an exceptionally large amount of money, and more than the entire amount spent on farm subsidies. Some say that the silver purchase program even destabilized the governments of China and Mexico.

Despite the confiscation of the silver owned by private citizens, the government still allowed silver coins to continue to circulate as currency. The amount of silver held in the Treasury peaked at 3.5 billion ounces, and by the early 1960s, silver had risen in price to $1.29 per ounce. Curiously, this is not because of scarcity, as had been intended by the buying up of silver, but because at $1.29 per ounce, the silver content in U.S. silver coins was equal to the face value. If the price of silver rose any higher, the general public could have taken their coins, even purchased further coins from any bank, and melted them down for a profit.

This new problem was dealt with by the government's selling silver to keep the price down. The public was not unaware of the problem that the government had, and many people took bank notes into a bank and collected silver change, which they stored as a secure source of value. To counter this action, the government started making coins with less silver content in 1965.

Later in the 1960s, government spending increased and fiat currency expanded to pay for the debts. Inevitably, this created inflation with the value of the dollar falling, particularly in relation to gold and silver. In other words, the price of gold and silver rose. People continued to hoard their silver as a result, which meant that many of the once widely used silver coins were taken out of circulation. Those same coins that were used to make purchases in the 1960s are worth about ten times their face value decades later because of the silver content.

Silver experienced a bull market in the 1970s that may be a precursor of the current times. Whenever there is a bull market, the value of silver seems to rise more quickly than gold, and arguably most of 2009 demonstrated a bull market at the moment. The price of silver soared from $1.63 per ounce in 1970 to $21.79 in 1979, an increase of over 1,200 percent. The last part of this increase happened swiftly in 1979, when people saw the increasing values and bought silver as quickly as they could. In the same period, gold went from $35.94 to $306.68, a mere 750 percent rise.

Human nature being what it is, during the 1980s many people continued to invest in gold and silver, despite the fact that it was now drastically overvalued. In the 1990s, investors were selling their precious metals, often at a loss, and buying up stocks, just in time for the crash of 2001. Following a trend is seldom so profitable as riding it while it is happening.

Back in the '60s, there was a lot of silver in circulation, and as mentioned above, the U.S. Treasury had billions of ounces in reserve. The currency of many countries included silver coinage, meaning it was even more plentiful. More or less, ever since that time the amount of silver held by governments has been reducing, as the governments sold off their silver inventories and began issuing coins using baser metals, or metals with less silver. The long-term effect of this has been that governments around the world are nearly out of silver, and the CPM Group estimates that total government holdings are now less than 50 million ounces. As mentioned, investors were also selling silver in recent times, and investor net sales are put at around 1.6 billion ounces from 1990 to 2005.

By now, you may be asking questions and wondering how governments can be short of silver, investors have sold off silver, and there is less silver in the world than there is gold. These facts all lead to a key difference between silver and gold, which is one reason why you cannot rely on the performance of one to be totally reflected in the performance of the other. Many experts would point to this difference as presenting the better opportunity for investing in silver than for investing in gold. At this stage, it seems that the general investing public may not be fully aware of the situation, which can give the informed investor a head start.

Where did all the silver go? The answer is that it went into consumer goods, a little bit at a time, because of the many uses of silver. The metal is a good electrical conductor, a good thermal conductor, and can be polished to be highly reflective. Silver has been used in photography for a long time, and the photographic process washes the silver down the drain, unless there is an arrangement to store and recover it. Silver used in brazing material for joining metals is essentially lost to the market. Silver used for biocides is dispersed. Whenever silver is used for many of the industrial processes, electroplating, batteries, and others, it is a small quantity of silver that is deposited or compounded and is essentially lost, unlikely to be recovered and reprocessed.

Of all of these uses, only coins, silverware, and jewelry keep the silver concentrated in one place and able to be used again. Virtually all the other uses for silver involve small, sometimes microscopic, amounts of silver that are used in components of other things, which are often thrown away when their useful life is done, like a battery. Contrast this to the life of gold — gold is mainly used for money and jewelry, and the estimates are that most of the gold that has ever been mined is still available somewhere.

Just to emphasize this point, here are some statistics about the reduction in silver over time. The U.S. Treasury held a peak of 3.5 billion ounces of silver in the '60s. By 1980 there were only 2.5 billion ounces of silver available to investors. By 1990, that had gone down to 2.1 billion ounces of silver. Increased industrial uses mean that silver stockpiles are virtually nonexistent. The U.S. Treasury's billions of ounces have dwindled to 20 million ounces, and it is a similar pattern in countries around the world. The fact that silver is no longer used in currencies for coinage means that it has largely disappeared without anyone really noticing. Data from the CPM Group shows that the amount of silver in the world could only cope with four months of consumption, if all production ceased.

In this century, silver has risen from around $4 per ounce to $23 per ounce at the time of this book's printing, with a peak of more than $23 per ounce in 2010. In the same time, gold has gone from $270 per ounce to the price of about $1,332 per ounce in October 2010, again rising more slowly than the price of silver. Traditionally, silver has been "the other one" — the less valued precious metal, and it is still thought of in the same way, which is why the general public seem slow to realize the scarcity.

THE FUTURE FOR SILVER

The answer to this may seem obvious. It is only necessary to ramp up the production of silver until there is a surplus, then technology can continue to prosper and supplies can be stock-piled against future events. The practicalities and economics of silver production conspire to make this unlikely to save the situation in the short term.

For example, most silver is extracted as a by-product of other mining activity. Unless the silver increases in value dramatically, it is just not worth the mining company's time to increase production. Silver might represent 1 percent of the income to a copper-mining conglomerate. Though that is nice to have, it is unlikely that overall production would be doubled just to get 1 percent more from the silver by-product. Unfortunately, 75 percent of silver production comes from such operations, thus there is little incentive at current pricing for this source to increase output.

The mines that have been established purely for silver production currently only produce 25 percent of the new silver each year, and that works out to a little over 100 million ounces. Even if production doubled instantly, it would take many years before the stockpiles were established.

Although it may not be possible to force double the production from existing mines, there is the alternative of opening more silver mines, ones dedicated to producing silver rather than those that produce it as a by-product. This is not a solution in the short term, and may be problematic in the longer term, too. It cannot help in the short term, as mines take a number of years to build and establish, even if the discovery has already been made. Given the current environmental laws, it can take much longer, or even not be allowed at all, depending where the discovery is. All this work needs to be funded, and the mining company manager would like some assurance that he or she would earn a good return from investing so much money up front. Unfortunately, at the moment silver prices are not sufficient to make it look economically viable for most operators.

Even assuming the economic problems are overcome, and the discoveries made and exploited, it still looks like silver will become a more valuable metal. The U.S. Geological Survey (USGS) has said in its annual mineral reports that it estimates there is less silver than any other metal available underground. At the current rates of production, it even calculates that we will run out of minable silver within 25 years.

WHAT CAN YOU BUY?

Like gold, silver comes in a variety of forms. You may want to invest in both physical and "paper" silver, and you will have numerous options for both types.

Physical silver can be bought as coins, "junk silver" bags, and bars or ingots. Silver is still incredibly inexpensive compared with gold, but as investors become aware of the bright future for silver, it may become virtually impossible to buy at a reasonable price. Take care to comparison shop when buying silver, and to only buy from reputable dealers. The same cautions apply to buying silver as were voiced for buying gold, and you should beware scams and opportunistic frauds.

Coinage

Arguably the most popular coins are the American Eagle silver bullion coins. Along with the American Eagle gold bullion coins, these were first minted in 1986. They are each 1 ounce of .999 pure silver, and they are created by private mints. As a result, the premiums for these coins are not large, and they can be bought for a cost not much more than the metal content value. This makes them an excellent choice for investors who are concerned to own physical silver for its metal value and want a convenient form for ownership.

The U.S. Mint announced in October 2009 that it would no longer be offering the American Eagle silver proof coin or the American Eagle silver uncirculated coin, both 1 ounce, citing unprecedented demand. The Mint is said to be working hard to make these coins available again in 2010. Public Law 99-61 directs the Mint to produce bullion coins in sufficient quantity to meet public demand, so all available the silver bullion blanks are being used to make the bullion coins, and not the numismatic versions.

It is also possible to buy 1-ounce rounds, which have the same weight and content as the American Eagle silver bullion coin. These rounds are not strictly coins, but are coin-like discs of silver that have been produced by private mints. Even without the face value of coins, they will always be worth the value of the silver contained in them. They are not as collectible and not as well-regarded, but they have a lower premium price than the American Eagle and are therefore a good choice for investors interested in the metal content.

For those people who are more concerned to invest in numismatic coins, which are more collectors items and include a large premium over the value of the metal content, there many choices. There are more silver coins than gold ones in existence. Until 1964, the silver coins in circulation contained 90 percent silver. From 1965 to 1970, the Kennedy half dollars were produced, containing 40 percent silver. Silver numismatic coins that you might consider investing in include:

- Morgan silver dollars
- Peace silver dollars
- Franken half dollars
- Early half dollars
- Liberty Seated quarters
- Roosevelt silver dimes
- Mercury dimes

"Junk silver" bags

These bags are anything but junk, even though they would be looked down on by collectors. The junk silver bag contains $1,000 worth of silver coins, taken at face value, which were issued prior to 1965. The name seems to have come about in the 1970s, the derogatory term being applied because the coins were at best in average circulated condition. The coins have been taken out of circulation and are generally in poor condition, which means collectors would not be interested in them. Nonetheless, for an investor who is interested in the metal content, they are an investment worth considering.

All the silver coins are 90 percent purity, but no rare coins are included. One of the selling points used to be that the bag could never be worth less than the $1,000 face value, regardless of what the silver price did. However, the bag weighs about 800 troy ounces (54 pounds) and contains about 715 ounces of silver, which is at least $12,000 at current rates, so it is very unlikely that you would have to rely on the face value in order to establish the worth. These are significant quantities of coins, either 4,000 U.S. quarters or 10,000 U.S. dimes.

It is interesting to note that you can also buy $1,000 face value bags of circulated coins with 40 percent silver, which is what the Kennedy half dollars were minted with between 1965 and 1970. Even with these, it is unlikely that you will ever have to rely on the face value in order to be able to spend them.

Silver bars and ingots

If you want to buy the most silver for your money, then bars and ingots work out better than buying coinage. They most frequently come in 100-ounce and 1,000-ounce sizes, and are stamped and numbered. They demand a very low premium over the spot price of silver.

Futures

As with gold, trading with futures on the metal can be a risky business and is not recommended unless you are prepared to commit time to studying the markets. Even then, there are issues that do not apply to gold. Traders in silver futures have "sold" a great deal of silver into the markets, perhaps in an attempt to manipulate the prices. In fact, the commodities traders on the New York Commodities and Mercantile Exchange (COMEX) have promised via futures contracts to deliver more than twice the amount of silver that is known to exist. In comparison, futures contracts on gold only promise about 2.5 percent of the current gold inventory. An interesting point about so much silver being sold "forward" is that it keeps the current price of silver low, creating "paper silver" out of nowhere. Anyone can benefit from this manipulation and buy silver at an artificially low price, which is neither reason investing in this metal is said to be on the rise, regardless of whether its investment vehicle is in physical or paper form.

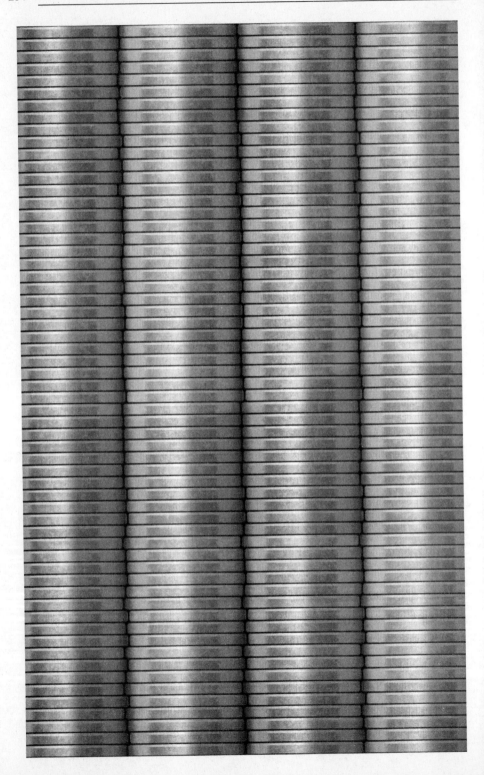

CHAPTER NINE

Other Metals

PRECIOUS METALS

Gold and silver are undoubtedly the metals that come to mind when you think of investing in precious metal. You can do very well by watching the markets and by buying these when the cycle turns and they are out of favor and undervalued, as they appear to be right now. If you are adventurous, or just plain curious, you may want to look at other precious metals that you can trade. The market for these is not as big, so liquidity is less, but they are still reasonable candidates for parts of your portfolio.

The other main precious metal that you hear about is platinum, and this represents the main alternative to investing in gold and silver. There are others that will also be briefly mentioned in the following pages.

Platinum

The value of platinum has been rising over recent years, and investors are starting to wake up to the possibilities for this alternative physical metal investment. Data from the CPM Group shows that the price was just over $400 per ounce in 2002 and peaked at $2,000 per ounce in 2008. It is now just over $1,680 per ounce, in October 2010. At one time platinum was much cheaper than gold, but now it is more expensive and looks like an excellent alternative investment.

Demand for platinum is increasing, with more industrial uses being developed for it. It is frequently used as a catalyst for chemical reactions. A catalyst enables and speeds up chemical reactions, but is not used up in them, so despite this widespread usage, the supply is not being depleted as quickly as you might think. It is used in the automotive and other industrial applications.

Platinum is also a beautiful metal used for fine jewelry. The trend for platinum jewelry grew through the '90s, but has now lessened. In the last couple of years, demand for platinum has flattened to around 7 million ounces, with more than half of that used in the automotive industry. The annual platinum supply is a bit more than the demand, and nearly 5 million ounces per year come from South African mines. However, the supply and demand figures do not tell the whole story, as there is little platinum stockpiled. If all supply ceased, then demand would use up the reserves of platinum within a year. Contrast this to the several decades worth of gold reserves, and platinum's demand can put it closer to the stand point of silver's demand.

When it was first discovered in South America by Spanish explorers in the seventeenth century, platinum was thought to be a nuisance, interfering with their mining operations for gold and silver. It was in Russia, where platinum was found in the gold fields in the early nineteenth century, that it was recognized as rare and valuable. The Russians made it into platinum rubles and minted nearly 500,000 ounces of platinum in 18 years, firmly establishing it as a store of value. Platinum is recognized for its beauty and strength and is valued much more highly than silver. It is still extremely rare, much rarer than gold, and if all the platinum mined throughout history were spread onto a football field, it would only be 3 inches thick.

The most popular forms of platinum bullion you can purchase include American Eagle coins and Canadian Maple leaf coins, as well as bullion bars. 10 ounce bars of .9995 purity are readily obtainable for about $13,000. There are four sizes of platinum American Eagle coins available, and they are all legal tender coins, although the metal content is worth far more than the face value. The largest is 1 ounce with a face value of $100, and this is the largest denomination coin ever issued in the U.S. The coin is also available in fractional sizes, with a half ounce at $50, a quarter ounce at $25, and one-tenth of an ounce with a face value of $10.

The platinum Canadian Maple Leaf coin was produced from 1988 to 2001 and was available as 1 ounce and smaller coins. The 1-ounce bullion coin has a face value of Canadian $50. It carries slightly fewer premium than the U.S. version, but either is a good way to invest in platinum metal.

Although not traded as widely as gold and silver, there are similar paper ways to invest in platinum. These include the indirect way of investing in mining stocks, which has many more aspects to it than just deciding on the right time to buy the metal. You should review the company's fundamentals in a similar way to those recommended for gold and silver if you intend to hold the shares for the long-term.

The same warnings apply if you choose to use options or futures with platinum or the other precious metals as they apply to trading derivatives in gold and silver. To become involved with either derivative, you should make yourself totally familiar with the risks and rewards, and be prepared to track the markets regularly for the best opportunities.

Palladium

Palladium is another white metal, not so well-known as platinum, and is mined as a by-product from platinum mines. It is similar physically to platinum and is also used in the automotive industry in catalytic converters. It has been less expensive than platinum, making it preferable for industrial purposes, and in general platinum and palladium compete with each other for similar uses. Palladium has been very volatile in price, reaching nearly $1,000 per ounce early this century, and most recently diving under $700. Investing in palladium is not for the fainthearted, but obviously with such swings in price, there are opportunities for great rewards.

At one time, palladium was regarded as inferior to platinum, and the price still reflects that notion. It is not been so widely adopted for jewelry yet, but there are some cutting-edge jewelers who are leading the field in palladium jewelry design. A breakdown of uses of palladium in 2008 include just over 1 million ounces for electrical, slightly less for dental, less again for petrochemical, and even less for jewelry. Of the 7.7 million ounces of palladium demand, by far the greatest amount, about 4 million ounces, was used in the automotive industry.

With regard to supply, this has been comfortably exceeding the demand in recent years. In 2008 there was a total supply of about 8.1 million ounces, with just over 2.5 million ounces each from South Africa and Russia, the largest producers.

Uranium

Because of its nature, uranium is often overlooked by investors. After all, not many people would seek to store radioactive material at home. But in terms of value, it is an exciting natural resource that will increasingly be demanded for energy-producing purposes. There are several possibilities that allow you to have uranium represented as part of your investment portfolio. There are several industrial applications, as well as the obvious military ones.

The military uses are controversial, and so are some civilian uses, given concerns with disposal of radioactive waste from nuclear reactors. Set against this is the energy crisis that is compelling much more serious consideration of nuclear generation facilities, even in countries and areas where activists have traditionally held sway. Uranium is used in producing about 16 percent of the world's electricity. Within another 15 years, it is estimated even today that there will be between 50 and 200 new nuclear plants built in the world, and the increasing energy crisis can only add to this figure.

Uranium — now and then

Uranium first became popular in the 1970s, and this heralded a bull market until the general public's fear started to turn people against it. In 1972, uranium cost less than $7 per pound, but by 1979 it was worth over $40 per pound. This was as high as it achieved in the bull run, and by 1980 the price started to fall due to unpopularity. The bear market lasted until the start of the new millennium, and in the year 2000 uranium could again be bought for less than $7 per pound because of the downward trend of the bear market.

Demand for uranium is continuing to grow overall, and mining it is becoming increasingly difficult. As with other precious metals, the most accessible supplies have already been mined, so it is only as prices increase that the more inconvenient and less accessible resources are tapped. Apart from this physical difficulty, by its nature uranium is subject to appreciable regulation, and there are a number of requirements that must be met before new mines can be started. The low price until the beginning of this century means that there is a lag in the exploitation of any new resources.

The demand for energy and new technology saw the creation of a new bull market for uranium, and at the start of the twenty-first century, supply could not keep up with demand. By 2007, it had soared to about $140 per pound and had seen a correction back to around $90 per pound — still considerably more than it had been just a few years earlier. The shortage of supply that drove the price hike was due to fewer above-ground supplies, the rising cost of oil, and generally rising demand. The correction was a response to a languishing economy and a reaction to the incredible increase in price.

The market for uranium has become confused in the recent year or two. Some countries are wholeheartedly embracing the idea of nuclear-powered reactors, and others are favoring less contentious solutions. Uranium is generally sold in the form of uranium-oxide concentrate, commonly called yellowcake, and this is the form that can be used to power reactors when converted, enriched, and formed into fuel rods. The prices have varied wildly for assorted reasons, but the underlying cause is that trading is difficult and illiquid — there is not enough buying and selling to allow consistent pricing.

Uranium investment

It is not feasible to own uranium as a physical product. There are several ways that you can take a financial interest in the market for uranium, and one of the most recent is with futures.

Since May 2007, uranium futures have been traded on the NYMEX. These are purely a speculative vehicle, particularly as they cannot be settled with the physical product, but are purely financially settled. In principle, they provide a trading place that can allow speculation on the price of uranium rising and falling, though with the disconnection between the futures markets and the physical metal, there is scope for some discontinuity between the two prices. The problem is that there is usually a link to the physical market, and the physical market will normally be traded with spot prices, and neither of these apply to the uranium futures.

You may also consider investing in funds that are related to uranium. For exposure to the price of uranium rather than other factors, such as involved in mining shares, you could consider buying shares in the Uranium Participation Corporation. This is an investment-holding company that is committed to use at least 85 percent of the investment to buy uranium. The goal is to follow the appreciation of uranium in a form that is easy for individual investors to take up. The price is volatile, reflecting the credibility of the physical material.

As with gold, you may choose to invest in stocks and shares of mining companies rather than in the physical material or a derivative of it. Also similarly to gold, you may expect that mining company shares will overreact to the price of uranium, increasing more than the amount that uranium goes up and declining more when it goes down. Add to this the volatility and uncertainty associated with this type of stock, and you may feel that this investment is too dangerous for your portfolio. You should be careful to allocate the degree of risk that you can tolerate and keep your financial interest down to an appropriate level.

Though uranium stocks are subject to the same influences as other mining stocks, there is another factor affecting the price: that of the price of oil. The more expensive oil becomes, with all other factors being equal, the better uranium stocks will perform, as they are part of the energy spectrum.

Another important aspect of uranium mining stocks is the geology of the areas where the mines are located, and you will find that the pricing is sensitive to the geography of the find. As with other mining, you have a basic choice of how well-developed the company is, and the exploratory mines are more speculative than the established mines with proven reserves. Political issues are a bigger concern with the perceived dangers of radioactivity, and the stability of the government in some countries may have a bearing on your decision.

In your research of the mining company, you will cover the basics, such as how long the area has been mined for uranium and what analysts' reports have been produced. For the speculative end of the spectrum, you may find little history and few opinions to advise you, mainly due to the exploratory nature of the business. As much as anything, you may need to establish an understanding of the experience of the principals involved and their backgrounds in order to decide whether to invest. At the other end, you may find that mining has occurred in the area since the last uranium boom, back in the '70s, so that the supply and reserves of ore are well-documented and the infrastructure in place.

OTHER PRECIOUS METALS

There are a few other less well-known metals that are counted as being in the platinum group, which are similar to platinum and have many uses in common. This group is less likely to be of general appeal, as there may be difficulties trading them with lack of liquidity. The generally smaller market for them means that they are likely to fluctuate more wildly and unpredictably than the major precious metals. If this is the sort of challenge you are looking for, then be careful that you have fully researched and are comfortable with trading in these metals.

- **Rhodium** is another by-product of platinum mining. The largest supply of rhodium comes from South Africa. Currently there are only about a quarter of a million ounces of rhodium mined every year, and it has seen prices as high as $6,000 per ounce recently. Its main use is as an alloy with other metals, including platinum and palladium. In common with these metals, it is used in catalytic converters and in electrical contacts.

- **Osmium** is a tough metal, with an extremely high melting point that is useful in a number of industrial processes. It can be alloyed with other elements to create metals that are extremely hard. It has also found a use in the manufacture of heart pacemakers and other medical devices.

- **Iridium** is exceptionally corrosion-resistant, said by some to be the most corrosion-resistant metal in existence. Amongst the better known metals, platinum used to have this title. Similarly to osmium, iridium can be used in alloy with other metals to make a stronger product, and it is also used in the manufacture of medical instruments.

- **Ruthenium** is perhaps the least well-known of the platinum group. The greatest supply of this metal is found in the Ural Mountains and in the Americas. It again has industrial uses, principally in strengthening other metals in alloy.

BASE METALS

Base metals are traded on the markets, and have mainly shown strength in recent years. The price of these metals is closely related to the performance of the economy, so they all dropped sharply at the end of 2008 and the beginning of 2009. For example, if the automotive industry is not doing well, as it was during the first part of 2009, then the demand falls and the price of some base metals will fall, too.

To counter this view in the longer term, you only have to note that many countries are now developing and wanting more consumer goods, which will put a squeeze on the existing and obtainable resources. The population of China and other emergent countries is becoming a major market force that cannot be ignored, and fighting — metaphorically — with other countries to get an increasing share of the raw materials is bound to lead to strengthening prices. The rate at which metals can be extracted cannot easily be increased quickly because of the capital investment and labor requirements. Unless there is a continuing period of higher prices, increased investment in mining may not be seen as cost-effective.

One of the huge benefits associated with base metals is their affordability, compared to the precious metals discussed previously. However, you must realize that base metal prices are much more economy-driven, and you need to learn of the uses of each to determine for yourself where increasing demand is likely to result in better prices. Where the "current" prices are quoted below, it is for the last quarter of 2009.

Aluminum

The past few years have seen volatility and an exciting time for the price of aluminum. It is commonly used in the transportation industry. You can find aluminum in the automotive industry, in aerospace, in housing, and in technological uses. More ways to apply aluminum are being discovered all the time, and the future demand looks quite strong. Over the past five years, aluminum has varied from 80 cents per pound in 2005 to peak at nearly $1.50 in the middle of 2008. It dropped to 60 cents per pound at the turn of the year, and now runs about 80 cents per pound. There is every reason to expect it to climb to at least the $1.30 range as the economy recovers.

Copper

Copper is one of the world's most widely used metals, and is found in practically all industrial applications. Despite some attempts by aluminum to invade the electrical industry for wiring, copper is clearly the favorite still in this application, and apart from any other uses, most industrial work requires electrical wiring.

The price fluctuations in the copper market have been much wilder than for aluminum, reflecting its dependence on the economical situation. Back in 2004, a pound of copper would cost about $1.40. Rising rapidly, from the middle of 2006 to the middle of 2008, copper traded in a range averaging around $3.50 per pound. The slump in 2008 saw copper back to its lower price, but now it is nearly $3 per pound again.

Lead

Lead has always had the reputation of being somewhat expensive, although expressed as a price per pound, the cost is seen to be fairly reasonable. As it is an extremely heavy metal, you do not get much volume to a pound. Consequently, it has been the target of thieves in the past, stealing lead from church roofs and taking lead piping.

Melting at a reasonably low temperature, lead has been used for molding into useful forms, and as it is malleable, it could be beaten into the necessary shape. At the current time, lead is used extensively for batteries. It is difficult to know how this usage will play out over the next few years — there is an increasing push in electric vehicles to reduce pollution, but there is extensive battery research to find more compact forms of batteries, so lead may or may not benefit from the green lobby.

Lead was priced below 50 cents per pound until the end of 2006, and shot up to around $1.70 at the end of 2007. There was a steady decline in spot price until the end of 2008, when it was under $.50 again, but in 2009 it climbed back to over a dollar per pound.

Nickel

The price of nickel increased in the early 20th century with the discovery that a small amount of nickel added to steel made an alloy that was much more durable. It is an essential component of stainless steel that has found increasing uses in the market. Because it is noncorrosive and has a high melting point, nickel is now used for many industrial purposes, mainly as a metal that is added to other metals to form a better alloy. It does not take a large percentage of nickel to change the basic properties of another metal.

The price chart for nickel in recent years is a little different from the other base metals. Certainly, it was low through 2004 and 2005, at around $6 per pound, a price to which it returned at the end of 2008 in the financial crisis. However, it peaked in the middle of 2007 at $24 per pound and rapidly lost value to around $13 per pound prior to the crisis. In 2009, nickel was back up to just $9 per pound.

Zinc

Zinc is used in a variety of industries, and like nickel, is combined with other metals to increase their noncorrosiveness. The majority of zinc is used in the automotive and construction industries, and in producing machines for industrial use. Its price pattern is similar to nickel, but it peaked earlier, at the end of 2006. It was 50 cents per pound in 2005, and again in the financial crisis, its peak value was $2 per pound; in 2009, it was around 90 cents per pound.

Although you may not have heard a lot about investing in metals like platinum, lead, or nickel, they are just a few of the options available to investors aside from the common metals, such as gold and silver. Each of the metals described in this chapter has multiple uses, allowing for more market fluctuation and increased diversification, presenting you, the investor, with more opportunities.

CHAPTER TEN

Tax Matters

You may justly be concerned that you comply with the IRS requirements when investing in gold and other precious metals. It is against the law to intentionally deceive or misreport any transactions in which the IRS has a declared interest, and there are stiff penalties for trying to cheat the revenue service out of their dues. Use the following information to determine what the IRS requires you to report.

REPORTING REQUIREMENTS

When you buy gold in any form for investment, you are not required to report this action to the IRS. Anyone who says that you need to is probably operating some sort of scam. For instance, an unscrupulous dealer may offer you a particular coin with the declared incentive that you do not need to report the purchase and the inference that you can keep your business secret, possibly avoiding taxes.

The only time there is any reporting of the transaction when you are buying gold or precious metals is when the value is $10,000 or more, and you pay with cash, or cash equivalents. This is for the obvious reason that such transactions can be used for money-laundering, involving drug dealing, terrorism, or other crime. Even then, you do not have to do any reporting, as it is the dealer's responsibility. To avoid the risk of loss, you would be wise to use a different method of transferring the funds anyway. A wire transfer is a safe and standard way of transferring funds and does not have to be reported.

When you sell gold, there are some items that the IRS requires details of, though they are not very clear. The IRS wants your dealer to file a Form 1099-B with them any time you sell:

- One or more gold bars weighing 1 kilo
- One or more gold bars weighing 100 ounces
- 25 or more Gold Maple Leaf coins
  (1 ounce of gold each)
- 25 or more South African Krugerrands
  (1 ounce of gold each)
- 25 or more Mexican Onzas (1 ounce of silver each)

Because the IRS rules are subject to interpretation, the Industry Council for Tangible Assets (ICTA) has issued further guidance for dealers. They assert that the dealer should report to the IRS if you sell:

- Any size gold bars totaling 1 kilo or more
- 25 or more coins as listed above
- Any size platinum bars totaling 25 ounces or more
- Any size palladium bars totaling 100 ounces or more

- Any size silver bars totaling 1,000 ounces or more,
- Any selection of silver coins, minimum 90 percent purity, totaling $1,000 face value or more

There is an exception for American Gold Eagles and Silver Eagles, and these do not have to be reported in any quantity.

If your sale results in a capital gain, then you are required to report this just as you would any other capital gain on items you buy and sell. Even if the dealer is required to report your sale under the terms outlined above, this does not relieve you from making your own tax return, including the capital gain. After all, it is not likely that the dealer will know how much you paid for the goods, so it is up to you to calculate your profit.

CASE STUDY: INDUSTRY COUNCIL FOR TANGIBLE ASSETS

```
Eloise Ullman
Executive Director
P.O. Box 1365
Severna Park, MD 21146-8365
(410) 626-7005

Diane Piret
Industry Affairs Director
P.O. Box 316
Belle Chasse, LA 70037
(504) 392-0023
```

Precious metals investors can avail themselves of the advantages of an individual retirement arrangement (IRA) in large part because of the efforts of the Industry Council for Tangible Assets (ICTA), which is a national trade association for investors and business people with a vested interest in precious metals, rare coins, and other numismatic and tangible assets. The ICTA worked with the Coalition for Equitable Regulation and

Taxation (CERT) to move forward federal legislation in 1997 that restored precious metals bullion as an acceptable investment for IRAs. In 1981, Congress removed bullion and coins as qualified individually-directed retirement plans. Until 1997, only U.S. American Eagles were acceptable as IRA-qualified precious metals investments. The efforts enabled IRA investors to reap the following benefits for precious metals:

1. Expanded qualified group of bullion products

2. Confirmed stated fineness that bullion products must meet to qualify

3. Ensured that primary market for mainstream and most liquid products were included

4. Enhanced retirement security through portfolio diversification

The ICTA continues its efforts to restore rare coins as qualified investments in IRAs and similar self-directed retirement plans. The ICTA works with CERT to do this.

Also, the association hopes that certain ambiguities can be resolved through their efforts. One such example is the unclear status of the distinction between an uncirculated and proof version of recently minted American Buffalo gold coins. Because the proof process identifies such coins as more strictly collectible than simply a bullion product, their inclusion in IRAs as acceptable metals is clouded.

If the ICTA can further the cause of investors and numismatists alike, eventually all U.S. coins will be treated alike and open for inclusion in IRAs. Rare coins like pre-1933 are not bullion and are most definitely collectible beyond their metal content alone. While such coins do not meet the fineness requirement for bullion, they still remain valued for their precious metal content, and the day may come when these coins also qualify for IRAs once again.

TAX EFFICIENCY

If you are not investing in gold directly, then you may wish to consult with your financial advisor to ensure that your affairs are arranged most tax efficiently. It is never against the law to try to avoid tax by means of your investments, whether it is through retirement accounts, trusts, or other means. It is only illegal if you try to evade tax — in other words, cheat on your taxes and intend to not pay that which is due.

For example, a gold fund may work out more tax efficiently for the U.S. resident than investing the same amount of money into a bullion-specific gold ETF (NYSE: GLD). The gains on the ETF would be taxed at the same rate as collectibles, such as gold coins, which is currently around 28 percent. In fact, if you sold in less than a year, you could be taxed at the maximum 35 percent rate. This is the same rate that would apply to bullion and numismatic coins. Thanks to some tax rate revisions, the current long-term capital gains tax rate is 15 percent, and this would be the rate applied to the gold fund, or to stocks, as long as they were held for more than one year.

When you are considering your investments for the long haul, you have a choice of how you will hold them. If you are looking on the investments as long-term, to possibly hold until retirement, you may want to make the investments through a tax-sheltered account, such as a retirement account. If, on the other hand, you are trading or investing for an earlier profit and intend to access any gains before retirement, then you must not use a retirement account; otherwise, you will be penalized when you withdraw the funds.

Regular account

Dealing first with a regular account, what you invest in and how long you hold it are important factors in how much tax is due. It is better to have a discussion beforehand with your financial advisor than to get to tax time and find that you could have made a different choice and saved money. Tax laws change, just as your personal finances will, so the advice that follows, while presented as accurately as possible at the time of writing, should not be considered personal financial planning advice.

With a regular account, you will generally be faced with four types of financial gain from the various financial instruments that you have invested in. These are:

- Long-term capital gains (over a year)
- Short term capital gains (less than a year)
- Interest payments
- Stock dividends

Long-term capital gains are subject to a lower tax rate than short-term gains, as these are regarded as more like income than capital appreciation. You will need to distinguish between these when you submit your tax information. Interest payments and stock dividends will be reported to you by your broker on tax forms 1099–INT and 1099–DIV, and these go on to lines 8 and 9 of the 1040 tax form, as currently printed.

As mentioned above, the problem comes when an item is taxed as a collectible, as some types of precious metals investments will be. You will need to check the current information to be sure of this, as the IRS changes its rules from time to time. At the moment, the items classified as collectible include bullion coins and bars, numismatic coins, and bullion-specific ETFs (GLD & SLV). The gains from these will be taxed at a higher rate, currently 28 percent for long-term gains and 35 percent if you have held them less than one year.

IRA account

Many types of precious metal investments are allowed to be held in an individual retirement arrangement (IRA). As you can see from the previous case study, the Industry Council for Tangible Assets prides itself that lobbying has opened the door to using an IRA for your investment.

The advantage of a traditional IRA is that you do not pay any tax on the money that you pay into it, and that you do not get taxed on any gains made by your investments within the account. You would normally choose to have any dividends and interest reinvested, and thus incur no current tax liability. If you have capital gains from buying and selling within the account, then no tax is due on those. In other words, your money grows tax-free until you take it for retirement income.

When you withdraw and use the funds from an IRA account in retirement, you are taxed on the income that you take out. As your overall income at that time is probably less than when you were working, the chances are that you will be on a lower tax rate, which is another gain for the IRA.

In order to get these benefits, there are a couple of major principles with which you must comply. First of all, you cannot take any money from the IRA until you are 59 ½, with just a couple of exceptions. If you find that you are forced to withdraw funds before then, the IRS will tax you heavily on them. They do not just charge back the tax you saved by investing in the IRA, and they also charge a penalty.

Secondly, there is a required minimum amount that you must take out, unless you want to be penalized. Your required beginning date is April 1 of the year after the year you were 70 ½. By that time, you should have taken the "required minimum distribution" from your IRA account; otherwise, there is a 50 percent tax penalty on the amount that you did not withdraw. The amount is available in tables from the IRS and is based on your age and life expectancy.

The current advice from the IRS can be found at their Web site, **www.irs.gov**. The latest advice as of October 2009 is dated 2008, and in summary says that a traditional IRA can be used to invest in collectibles. The downside is that the amount invested is "considered distributed to you in the year invested." According to the rules that apply to retirement accounts, if you take a distribution from the account before you are qualified by reason of age, then you may be assessed tax. This stems from the fact that retirement accounts have tax-favored treatment just because the funds in them are not meant to be touched until that time — they cannot be used as a general tax-saving vehicle with free access when you decide to use the money.

Currently, the list of collectibles given by the IRS includes:

- Coins
- Stamps
- Gems
- Books
- Jewelry
- Sports memorabilia
- Dolls
- Certain other tangible personal property, (not including art)

They provide an exception, which allows that an IRA can be invested in U.S. gold coins weighing one, one-half, one-quarter, or one-tenth of an ounce, and silver coins of 1 ounce, only minted by the U.S. Treasury. The exceptions also include "certain platinum coins" and "certain gold, silver, palladium, and platinum bullion." The fact that this is called an exception presumably means that these are not subject to the distribution rule associated with collectibles, although this is not made clear from the instructions.

CAPITAL GAINS AND LOSSES

The chance are, particularly the way the 2009 market shaped up, that most of your investment gains are going to be capital gains. Any time you buy something at a certain price and sell it later for more, you have made a capital gain, which simplistically is the difference between the two prices. There is a lot more to the topic, and ways to minimize the amount that you owe the IRS for making a profit.

As mentioned above, there are two types of capital gains: short-term and long-term. The short-term gains apply when you have held the asset for a year or less before selling it, and the long-term gains apply to anything more than one year. Short-term gains are taxed at a higher rate because they are regarded as income by the IRS. The greater your short-term gains, the higher tax rate you may be exposed to, as rates increase with your income.

Long-term capital gains are much more favorably treated by the tax payer. The tax rate is far lower, which means if you have a choice of selling an asset after 11 ½ months or after 12 ½ months, the decision is easy, with all other factors being equal.

Capital gains are calculated from the selling price and what is called the "basis," which is often what you paid for the asset. The basis includes an allowance for additional money you may have put into the asset. For instance, if you buy and sell a house, you are allowed to add any costs for improvements onto the buying price to establish a higher basis price, which gives a smaller capital gain reflecting the profit that you actually made. In the case of investments, if you pay a commission when you buy, then you can add that to the price you paid to get the basis.

Sometimes you will not make gains, but will have losses when you sell investment property. You can use these losses to offset the gains and reduce your tax liability. It is important to note that capital losses are only allowed on investments, and not on personal property. If this were not the case, then you would be able to claim many losses on items like your car or television when you sold or traded them in, and this would not achieve the objective of taxing you.

Once you have calculated your net long-term capital gain, you are allowed to deduct your net short-term capital loss to get your net capital gain, on which you pay tax at the rate of 15 percent, or 28 percent for collectibles in the year 2008. From 2008 to 2010, some gains may be taxed at 0 percent. However, if your capital losses are more than your capital gains, then the excess can be taken off your income on your tax return, up to a limit of $3,000 each year. If your losses are more than this, then the unused part is carried forward to your next tax year.

Full details of capital gains and losses treatment for investments are given in IRS Publication 550, Investment Income and Expenses (Including Capital Gains and Losses).

Chapter Eleven

But is it for You?

Up until this point, you have read details of why gold and gold-related securities may prove to be a rewarding investment, and been presented with facts to support that view. You have been made aware of the benefits, risks, and pitfalls of the various financial instruments discussed, and may have formed an opinion on what if any type of gold investing would suit you.

Now is the time when you need to review your financial situation, your motivations for researching this topic, your resources and your abilities, and determine if making some investments in gold is the right choice for you. Although some of the investment opportunities reviewed are said to have more risk than others, remember that risk is relative. Some would say that investing in the physical metal is less risky than leaving money in a bank account, as that is guaranteed to depreciate through inflation, whereas gold may retain its value and be worth more dollars in the long run.

If you go back to the basics, you may form a clearer picture of what you need to achieve with your money, and this may point you in the direction of the best investments for your situation. Money is, after all, only a means of exchanging work and property to facilitate the process of living. Investment is a means to an end, whether that is to safely increase your cash value for an earlier or more adventurous retirement, or whether you intend to pass on a wealthy estate to your heirs to ease their monetary concerns. Perhaps you are a gambler and looking for a few big lucky breaks to change the course of your life, content to make do if the breaks do not happen. Most likely you are in between, wishing that a lucky break would happen along to make things easier, but not wishing to forgo a comfortable retirement by risking too much on that option.

It is easy to become excited when you realize the opportunities that gold investing offers, and commit too much of your portfolio to pursuing them. With the best of research and analysis, there is an element of risk in most forms of investment. In some, it is mainly the risk of timing, where you can have confidence that the value of your investment will not vanish but may fluctuate and dictate the appropriate time to cash out; in others, the risk is a real threat to your capital with a small chance of losing much of it in exchange for the opportunity to make more.

So before you commit to the concept of putting everything you own in gold and riding it up for a large profit, you need to take a look at your financial situation and see to what extent you can afford to do this. You need to get your financial house in order before investing money that you may require urgently for an emergency, for instance.

1. Have you been prudent with your financial affairs?

2. Do you usually have a balance on your credit cards that lingers before finally getting paid off? You may want to hold off on investing because the cost of interest on a credit card will take money away from your investment reserve.

3. Have you paid off your mortgage? With a reasonable rate of interest and tax benefits, you should be able to come out ahead by keeping your mortgage and just using spare cash or funds for your investments.

4. Is your car on loan? If so, is it a zero-interest rate loan? In recent years, these types of loans have allowed investors to maintain their loan on the car and still invest.

5. Do you have money set aside as needed for items like emergencies, bills, and other expense? You need to have some cash on hand for emergencies. Depending on your view, you may want a supply of dollar bills, or you may be happy to have a cash equivalent, such as a money market fund, where the money can be accessed fairly easily. The old advice used to be to have six months' worth of expenses available to cover any unforeseen job losses or accidents. Some people have been tempted to increase that amount because of considerations about job security, but if you have six months' worth available, you are doing better than most people. If you are out of work, there will be job search costs, but you should be able to save by cutting out regular commuting and other items of expenditure.

6. Have you purchased, or set aside money, for nonperishable goods and food to protect you from any aftermath that could result from a financial misfortune?

After you have taken care of all these items, then any spare money you have left over can be put to financial good use. But consider the following questions to allow you to focus on your approach to life:

- How involved do you want to be in your investments each day? Are you content to rebalance your portfolio a couple of times a year; do you want to review it every few weeks; or are you looking for a trading situation, where your frequent attention to the performance of the market may help to boost your profits?

- How old are you, and how soon will you be needing to use the money that you are investing? If you are young and looking to the long term, are you intending to make regular investments to increase your retirement account?

- Are you looking to make investments that will give you a regular income, to supplement or replace your ordinary income? Do you want to lock away your investment without touching it for living expenses, allowing the value to compound until a certain time in the future?

- What level of involvement with your investment would allow you to sleep well at night? Unless you prefer insomnia, your disposition toward risk is a very important part of the consideration for your investment capital. You may have clues toward your attitude from previous investment opportunities, where you may have found you can tolerate a measured chance without problems, or you may have been concerned enough that you checked your investment performance of every opportunity, just to make sure that nothing had gone wrong. Only you will know your feelings.

Just as you focused on your propensity for risk and expectation of returns, now you must focus on what the various gold investment vehicles can do for you. What are their risks and returns? First of all, you must recognize that precious metals are primarily a way to preserve wealth — or in the face of an inflationary fiat currency, to achieve capital appreciation. Buying and holding a piece of gold, no matter how many times a day you look at it, will not generate any income for you. If you buy physical gold, you should be looking for the long-term, and not looking to get access to any of the funds you commit for a while. This is even more true if you choose to buy coins, as you will be paying a premium over the value of the weight, even if you buy bullion coins. Unless you hold these for several years, your returns, when you sell, will be disappointing.

There is no such thing as a sure thing, but it sure looks like this thing — an increasing price of gold — will happen over the coming years. With physical gold, provided you do not lose it and it is not stolen, there is little risk; all you have to do is take care of the security, wherever it is held, and you will be able to sleep like a baby.

The case for gold and other precious metals is reinforced by the current financial crisis. There is a finite quantity of these, and even the metal still in the ground is limited and will cost an increasing amount to extract, as mining companies will have to develop less rich seams. Physical gold is an excellent prospect for a conservative portfolio. It stops short of being guaranteed — witness the surge in price that happened a couple of decades ago and is only now being matched — but every indication is that we are not in that situation now.

The situation can change if you look at trading in gold-related securities in order to develop an income stream. First, there are ways that you can generate income without exposing yourself to a large amount of risk. You can look for a mining stock that has good fundamentals and is solid, and also pays dividends. You may also look at buying bonds in a mining company and receiving interest, although at the current low interest rates, this would not seem to be a good move. If you have bonds that pay low interest, and the interest rate in general rises, then the value of the bonds will go down.

The other method of developing an income stream from stocks is with the covered call, and this is a very under-utilized device. Most investors research the stocks that they buy with reasonable care but give little thought to actively creating additional income from owning them. As covered in the options section of Chapter Five about the stock market, in the best case this will keep generating income while you keep selling successive calls, and this income will be much better than simple capital growth. If the shares are called away from you because the option becomes in the money, then it is true you do not get paid the current increased market value for them. You will, however, still get more than you paid for them, if this is how you have been selling your calls, with them "out of the money." If you aim to produce income and incur little risk, this method deserves your attention.

When trying to match your goals and temperament to the investment vehicle that suits you, remember that the amount of risk you are willing to assume does have bearing on the returns you can expect. By clever use of the facilities at your disposal, you can change the risk, as with the covered call, but there is a general relationship between the two.

To protect yourself from risk, you may consider diversifying your investments. Diversification can take three forms: by investing in different markets, different positions, and in different investment vehicles. The market is subject to some new threats, such as terrorism, which serve to make it more volatile than it used to be. Mass communication and instant messaging and blogs serve to inform investors simultaneously at the mention of a problem, and this can have a marked effect on a security, which means your investment should be in several different financial instruments. For instance, you may want to have some investments in stocks, some in futures, and perhaps some junk silver. If the stock market is having a bad day, you will still have the futures and junk silver. If the futures market takes a turn for the worst, then you have your stocks and physical metal to reassure you.

Although gold and other precious metals may appear strong, you must diversify into other market sectors in order to retain your protection. The old advice used to be that about 10 percent of your portfolio should go into gold and gold-related investments. Many experts are advising more than this in the bull market for gold. Though some would argue for more, it is reasonable to have a limit of about 30 percent gold-related investments, even in a market with an upward trend. Any more than that would be speculation. You should never forget that gold has shown volatility in the past, plunging from $725 per ounce in May 2006 to well below $600.

GOLD BULLION AND BULLION COINS

If you want to buy gold as insurance against a catastrophe, then there is no better way than to buy physical gold that you can keep in your possession. Though complete failure of the banking system is unlikely, an increasing number of banks are finding that the FDIC is having to move in on them due to their financial situation, and this situation may become worse in time. If the possibility of this happening is one of your reasons for holding gold, then you will need to take steps to secure the metal within your reach, as a safety deposit box at a bank may not be easily accessible.

It is important that you buy bullion coins based on their gold content, and the premiums for them should be small. They are a different sort of investment vehicle from numismatic coins, and it is far easier to readily recover your investment when you have the value of the metal making up the majority of the price. When the Krugerrand was introduced in the 1960s, South Africa was unpopular, and therefore the Krugerrand had to be sold with a low premium to attract any buyers. This had the effect of forcing down the premiums charged on other gold coins, but the Krugerrand is still about the lowest you will find.

Some dealers may try and influence you to buy Canadian Maple Leaf bullion coins by emphasizing the purity of the gold used, which is 99.99 percent or 24 carats. While these coins are an excellent investment, there is no particular reason to buy them for the purity of the gold. If you buy 22-carat gold coins, they will be valued on the basis of the gold content, in this case 91.6 percent, so it will make no difference. Pay attention only to the premium over the gold value.

An investment in bullion bars is less likely to be useful in the event of a systemic breakdown of the financial system, purely because bullion bars are much heavier than coins and cannot be used easily for everyday spending. A small bar is anything under the 400-ounce London Good Delivery bars, so it may still be many thousands of dollars' worth of gold. The smallest bars will have a higher premium than large bars, which leads to a preference for bullion coins.

The chief risk in owning an investment of this type is that of loss or theft. When making your purchase, you should try to time the market to make sure you get the best deal, but if you see that gold prices are on a run upward, it may be best to buy and go with the trend.

Numismatic and collectible coins

If you are interested primarily in gold investing because of the expected future for gold prices, then you may wish to avoid buying proof coins and the newly issued coins and commemoratives. You may expect that all of these trade at quite a high premium over the value of the metal content, perhaps costing double. Often you will find that they are available at a lower price a few years later. If the market is such that you are not paying a large premium over the value of the content, then they may be considered a good prospect.

With that in mind, there is a large market for numismatic coins, and they attract many avid collectors. Provided you research your particular investment, you will be able to identify the coins that are in demand and find good investments from a collectible standpoint. Collectibles in all fields are generally having a bull market, and that includes fine art and other physical items. Joseph Barrett is keen to explain the appeal in the following case study:

CASE STUDY: JOSEPH M. BARRETT

Joseph M. Barrett - Owner/Numismatist
Cincinnati Rare Coin Galleries
Offices in Fairfield, Hyde Park, & Milford
4942 Dixie Hwy
Fairfield, Ohio 45014
513-892-2723
Hosts "Coin Talk" Sundays 9 p.m. 55KRC in Cincinnati
www.mainstreetcoins.com
mcoins@cinci.rr.com

As a rare coin retailer and collector at heart, I can tell you that the fusion of businessman investor and hobby enthusiast is invigorating when gold coins are involved. From childhood, when Grandpa "plucks" that first half dollar from behind our ear, we seem conditioned to pursue coins. Perhaps money in general, sure, but we always seem to find ourselves in possession of those pieces we got in change on our first date, or that first dollar made. Time spent spinning an old silver dollar on one's desk and considering for a moment where that dollar has been is not time wasted; it is a well-spent homage to our past. We tend to keep our money close; it is no surprise we feel so close to our ancestors when holding the money.

Anyone with a modicum of investable income can reap the rewards of this hobby/investment, especially through the availability of pre-1933 gold coins issued by the U.S. government prior to the gold recall confiscation order by then-President Franklin D. Roosevelt. These pre-1933 U.S. legal tender coins comprise the core of rare gold-coin collecting today. Their appeal is enhanced by their age and history of these most widely recognized coins that were minted as dollars, quarter eagles, half eagles, eagles, and double eagles, with the "eagle" equivalent to $10 at the time.

The readily identifiable gold content of these U.S. antiquities provides a metal baseline for their value, but other factors such as condition play a large role. One should note that all coins are graded on a 1 to 70 scale, and in most cases, the higher grades will command the highest premiums. This condition is sometimes ensured by sending the coin to a third-party grading service, where the coin is encapsulated and a grade is indicated on the holder. Mintage figures and date/mint mark combined most definitely contribute to the collectible value of these coins as well. Owning a gold piece from the now nearly forgotten mints in Charlotte, Dahlonega, and Carson City is rewarding and valuable in ways other than owning a piece strictly for its high grade or low mintage. Because of these factors and other issues, I absolutely recommend two first steps for would-be rare gold coin collectors/investors:

1. **Buy the book and then buy the coin.** Coin collecting is a phenomenal hobby, and much information must be weighed before targeting what types of coins are most appealing for each individual collector.

2. **Ally yourself with a dealer.** Reputable dealers have considerable experience and resources. Their collector services can help you determine which coins suit your interest best, as well as locate and arrange the purchase of coins for you; this is the role of every professional numismatic dealer.

MUTUAL FUNDS

When you want to invest your money in a certain sector of the market but know that you do not have enough time or knowledge to choose the investments carefully, then you should think of mutual funds. Mutual funds just use the collected assets from many investors to invest in stocks. They have the advantage that they are run by professional managers, whose job in life is to make stock selections and keep up with the news, so they are ideal for the busy investor. As they invest so much money, there is the advantage of diversification for the individual.

One general disadvantage they have had until recently was that they were very limited in their investment strategies. Unlike hedge funds, they are strictly regulated and so were not able to take advantage of all the derivatives and other financial instruments that hedge fund managers could enjoy. In particular, they could not take a short position on any stocks — that is, to invest so as to profit from the price falling. This situation is gradually changing, and the worlds of hedge funds and mutual funds are drawing closer. Creative mutual fund managers are able to take advantage of many opportunities.

A point worth noting is that you can assign the mutual fund shares to your IRA or 401(k) plan, and legally get around the problem that you cannot put bullion in a tax favored savings account. Mutual funds are available that invest in the metal or in mining shares and, as mentioned previously, the shares enjoy a leverage over the price gains of the metals, so these funds will do well in a gold bull market.

The risk with mutual funds is that they are not so easily traded as shares or ETFs, so you are not able to follow the day-to-day movements of the market and depend on the manager's expertise to avoid losses. In the financial crash of 2008/2009, mutual funds lost money; because they do not employ many hedging techniques, they tend to follow the market. In fact, mutual funds usually gauge how well they have performed by comparison with the relevant market index — so if the S&P 500 were down 40 percent and the equivalent mutual fund were down 30 percent, curiously the fund manager would claim to have done well.

EXCHANGE-TRADED FUNDS

Perhaps you should consider investing in ETFs. This relatively new investment vehicle has become popular, as it seems to combine the best points of the market. If you are not so conservative, the ETF provides investment potential that is probably best compared with mutual funds rather than stocks, even though ETFs can be traded throughout the day. Like mutual funds, ETFs are diversified packages of stocks or bonds, and you can buy them throughout the trading day like a regular stock.

As with the best mutual funds, ETFs have low expenses. However, they are much more flexible, as they do not have minimum holding requirements and do not charge redemption fees. Many people feel that they are the best investment vehicle available for anyone wanting to become involved in stocks and shares. Most ETFs are actually based on index funds, which provides diversification for your money.

As mentioned in Chapter Five, ETFs are also available that are based on the price of gold (GLD) and the price of silver (SLV), effectively allowing you to trade on the rise and fall of the physical metals. The ETF companies actually own allocated gold, which means that the physical metal, complete with serial numbers, is held in the vaults. This does not mean that you own the gold, but merely that you have a claim on the company for the gold. The gold is the property of the fund.

The positive side of ETFs for "buying" the metals is that you can invest what you want, and buy and sell during the trading day, paying only a commission to your stockbroker. The investment has all the protection that you get from trading on a regulated market, so you will not be involved with dealers you have not dealt with before.

The negative side is that you do not actually own the metal and are dependent on the financial system. If you believe that this may break down at some time in the future, then you would be exposing yourself to a crash from which you may be unable to withdraw the money.

FUTURES CONTRACTS

Futures contracts involve leverage, and they involve risk. Depending on your disposition and approach, this may delight you or may terrify you. Dealing in futures contracts is certainly something that should not be entered into lightly, and no matter how well-informed or skilled you are, it is important that any money you use for this purpose is nonessential money, set aside for speculative trading.

Having said that, provided you are not scared that the financial system is going to collapse completely, you may be interested in the benefits that you can achieve with leverage available on futures contracts. If you are interested in short-term positions, rather than long-term buy-and-hold strategies, it may be worth your while looking into this option. If you are taking up a speculative stance, be advised that your best course is to "paper trade" for a time to see how you do. Paper trading involves writing down what you would do with your money in real-time and keeping account of the ups and downs that the imaginary investment experiences. Frequently, you are able to open a demonstration account with a broker, which will allow you to actually enter the intended trades and see how they would have performed.

GOLD MINING SHARES

As Warren Buffett says, you should only buy shares in businesses that you understand. If you are not able to spend the time to understand the mining industry, then you may be better off investing in a fund that has an informed manager making those decisions. The mining industry, unlike some others, requires specialist knowledge in scientific areas such as geology and mining equipment.

That said, if you are prepared to work at understanding the company reports and particularly the survey information, there is a tremendous upside available for the investor in mining shares. As pointed out previously, many of the costs involved with operating a mine are fairly constant, so an increase in the price of gold can be reflected many times over in the price of the shares. In view of the bullish gold market that exists nowadays, the downside — that a fall in the price of gold decimates profits and share value — is not so likely.

You must be prepared to analyze each company individually until you find one that satisfies your criteria for risk and reward. Unlike investing in the physical metal, your selection between the various companies and means of investing is critical, and it spells the difference between success and failure. Size of company and stage of development of their mines is crucial. There are few feelings to compare with discovering a small exploratory company, investing in the penny shares, and watching as their dreams come true and the company expands.

With a bull market, early on there will be rapid growth in the shares of the largest mining companies, the blue-chip stocks, as they have low production costs and are established. They represent the next-safest thing for the investor who is looking for some exposure to gold beyond the physical metal.

As the market progresses, medium-size companies become more profitable or just come into profit, and they are worth looking at right now, as gold starts its run. They are still more risky than the blue chip companies, but they carry with them a greater potential for profit.

Finally, and only if you are prepared to face the greater risks, as gold increases in value the smaller companies become more viable, and present the chance of the largest returns. In some cases, the return can be multiples of the initial investment. If you want to go down to this level of company, be careful in your research and check out the résumés of the principals. If you can identify several good prospects, then at the share prices these companies trade, you should be able to diversify your holdings across different mining companies and global regions to minimize the risk.

Apart from your research into the companies, be sure that you look into the political situations and the governments of the countries where the mines are located. A company can be stifled by an uncooperative operating environment, and even good fundamentals cannot succeed against onerous new regulations.

GOLD FUNDS

More secure than investing on your own in mining shares, gold funds provide an opportunity to be exposed to profit from gold's rise in price. While some shares may tank even while gold is increasing because of bad management or being in the wrong place, the gold fund manager has access to the necessary research to be sure he or she is invested in the most promising areas with the best-run companies.

When you are selecting a fund in which to put your money, there are several factors that you should check into so that you can be sure to get the best returns. You may do your research from published performance in financial newspapers such as the *Wall Street Journal*, and **www.MorningStar.com** is a useful resource for looking into fund performance. By exercising due diligence, you should be able to minimize your risk.

Look for the statement of fund objectives to be sure that the fund aligns with your aspirations. Keep in mind that some funds will be more speculative, with the possibility of greater returns, and do not expect that a high-growth approach to investing will be as secure as the fund that tends toward investing in established, large mining companies.

While the mining fund manager may not be able to control the markets and the return from the shares held by the fund, he or she is able to control the expense ratios, loads, and any other costs. A highly managed fund is likely to have higher costs than a fund that invests in large companies and holds the shares for a long time, so you must make sure that you compare like with like when looking at costs.

You will also be interested in the number of assets in the fund and how much trading is done — that is, the portfolio turnover. With a high portfolio turnover, you may find you are paying more tax because of capital gains realized by the fund.

There is an excellent Internet resource for those interested in gold funds, and that is Eagle Wing Research at **www.eaglewing.com.** They publish a guide to gold funds and give access to a limited amount of free information for all investors. They monitor 22 leading U.S. gold funds, and will give you a starting point from which to make your own research. If you wish, you can also subscribe to obtain further information on the funds before making your choice.

Comparison of ways of investing in gold				
Product	*Minimum investment*	*Skill level*	*Potential profitability*	*Degree of risk*
Gold bullion	High	Low	Good	Low
Gold bullion coins	Low	Low	Good	Low
Numismatic coins	Low	Medium	Good	Medium
Digital gold	Low	Low	Good	Low
Mutual funds	Low	Medium	Good	Low
ETFs	Low	Medium	Good	Medium
Gold funds	Low	Medium	Good	Medium

Junior mining shares	Low	High	Excellent	High
Midsize mining shares	Low	High	Excellent	High
Large mining shares	Low	High	Very good	Medium
Options	Low	High	Excellent	Varies depending on use
Futures	Low	High	Excellent	High

CONCLUSION

As you can see, investing in gold may be a very opportune thing to do right now, and there are many different ways that you can do that using the amount of money you have and suiting your appetite for risk. Timing of investments is often an issue with people, and perhaps it is wise to take a larger view of this particular market sector. After all, it is quite possible that there will be a correction right after you buy in to your chosen gold related security. Be prepared for what may happen. The markets seldom cooperate or do what they should do, and sometimes a simple acceptance of this can make any negative experience tolerable.

At the time of writing, in October 2010, the price of gold has hit a new record, and the immediate target is $1,400 per ounce. By the time you read this it may have passed that level, and the next target level will be $1,400 per ounce. Within a year or two gold may pass the $2,000 barrier. The fundamentals are sound, and we are not in the situation experienced in 1980, when a high price was inevitably followed by a slump.

In looking at what could forestall this rise in the price of gold, there are three factors that have an influence:

1. Inflation is expected to follow the bailouts and economic recovery plans that have demanded so much fiat currency spending. This is simple economic theory — if there is more printed money in circulation, and basically the same amount of goods and services, there is little else that can happen, except that everything becomes more expensive. The realization of this is one of the factors contributing to the interest in gold investing and subsequent increasing price. It is unlikely that this will continue in a smooth relationship. Inflation has not taken off as much as was feared, and at some stage the public perception may be that it is not such a threat, and interest in gold will wane, allowing the price to reduce.

2. The economic crisis is a driving force for people to flee to the traditional security of owning gold. Such activity we have witnessed in the last year. There is the possibility that, with careful government control being exercised and ongoing public relations, it will appear that the financial system is under control and has returned to normal business. Though there are fundamental problems that challenge the way that government and commerce have been run in recent decades, if the public perceive that business is back to normal, then that there may be a reversion from

gold to the stock market, which would cause gold to hesitate in its rise.

3. Looking at the technical analysis, it is possible that gold will suffer a downward correction. The last four times that the gold price spiked up towards or through $1000 per ounce, it quickly retreated for a while. Psychological factors play an important part in trading, and $1,000 is a huge milestone. It may be that the market is not ready to accept continued pricing exceeding $1,000 at the moment.

These three factors will have been tested by the time this book hits the market, and the answers to these questions will be clear.

In case you are wondering, there seems little chance that it will go up to a value that will allow the U.S. to revert to the gold standard, as it may have been possible in the 1980 boom. Although the government has ceased to publish the M3 figures showing the amount of money in circulation in recent years, presumably from embarrassment, estimates are that the price of gold would have to touch nearly $40,000 per ounce in order for the reserves to cover the printed currency.

If you are interested in keeping up with the news of gold, then research information on the Internet. There are several free newsletters available and many subscriptions, some of which you will be offered when you sign up for the free information. Agora Financial is a major publishing group that has some interesting products, and their free newsletter *The Daily Reckoning* is worth looking at. You can sign up for it at **www.dailyreckoning.com**.

Along with gold, there is a strong case for considering adding silver to your portfolio. Although often grouped together, gold and silver have a very different backgrounds and applications, and should be treated as separate cases when considering the merits of investment. Silver appears to be more speculative overall, but there are many aspects making up that summary judgment.

The production of silver continues whether or not the market is there, as most silver is produced merely as a by-product of other metals' extraction. This means that even in periods where the price of silver was low, silver was still being produced and stockpiled. It also means that it is more difficult to increase production just to bring more silver into the market, as that is a marginal benefit to the mining company.

As has been explained, the uses of gold and silver could not be more different in many aspects. The fact is that most gold that has ever been produced is still in existence and identifiable. Silver is the opposite. As pointed out, we are nearly running out of silver and production cannot cope with the demand. Silver is lost in many of the applications for which it is well-suited. The fact that so many industrial applications now rely on the use of silver means that it will continue to be sought after until it is uneconomic to use in that way, when it is to be expected that other techniques will be developed. These will take time, and the shortage of silver is likely to impact the price significantly.

Although the price of gold can be artificially regulated by governments buying and selling, as has occurred several times in the past, silver has no such safety net. The reserves held by central banks around the world are minimal, which precludes selling to maintain a reasonable price. Perhaps the most frightening aspect of the silver shortage is the number of future contracts that have been sold, which covers far more than all known available silver. While undoubtedly this may in part be a price manipulation exercise, it seems that there is no easy resolution to it. This is for another very clear difference between gold and silver. Gold futures are mainly speculative, and silver futures have substance and need delivery.

Many of the buyers of a "long" silver futures contract do not do so for speculative profit reasons, but because they are industrial manufacturers who will need the metal for their products. This is the traditional purpose of a futures contract — locking in the supply of a commodity at sometime in the future to avoid the ups and downs of the spot market. Many traders of futures seem to assume that settlement in money is all that is required, and so they are content to speculate on whatever commodity appears to give them the best chance of a profit.

Warren Buffett bought 139 million ounces of silver a decade ago using futures contracts. When he demanded delivery, none was available. He had to sue in order to receive the silver. He has now sold his silver, and in retrospect admitted that he sold it too soon. With outstanding futures contracts for far more than the amount of silver available, and a commodity market with a bias toward physical delivery, one can only assume that at some time not too far in the future, there will be massive shortages and soaring prices. If it was just about the money, then simple bankruptcy or bailout could provide the answer. As it is about the manufacture and availability of many products that we use in present-day society, there admits no easy solution, and silver appears poised for a massive increase.

Regardless of the type of metal you choose to invest in, many Wall Street experts are turning to precious metals as a means of diversifying and securing portfolios. With the intrinsic value of gold marking its popularity since ancient times, the metal continues to be a sound investment because of its many forms and uses. With advancements of technology, investing in more abstract forms of gold is also an option, especially as the price of gold continues to rise.

If the price of gold does rise as may be expected, then in the future you may want to watch out for the possibility that irrational enthusiasm could push the price higher than it can be justified by fundamental economics. It is in the nature of the general public to jump on a trend after it has started running, and to continue supporting and chasing the trend, even when it should have ceased. As with the gold price spike in 1980, it is quite possible that the price will overshoot and suffer a large correction, and you should be ready to take what may be appreciable gains at that time rather than hanging on to your gold as it slides back. According to industry experts, gold should easily clear $2,000 per ounce, but many experts believe that it will not continue beyond this. Still, in times of economic hardship, gold provides a solid investment for both the small and large investors who are looking to diversify in a low- or high-risk setting.

Appendix A

Just the Facts

Weights and measures	
1 troy ounce	= 1.097 ounces avoirdupois
Gold is measured in troy ounces, which are a little different from the ounces in common use, which are called avoirdupois	
1 pound	= 16 ounces
1 short ton	= 2,000 pounds
1 metric tonne	= 2,204 pounds
	= 32,151 troy ounces

Purity of gold		
	Parts per 1000	*Use*
24 carat	1,000 (theoretical)	Pure gold, too soft for jewelry
	999.9	Also called "four nines" gold
	995	Adequate for London Good Delivery
22 carat	916	Common for Middle Eastern jewelry
18 carat	750	Common for European jewelry
14 carat	583	Common for the U.S.
10 carat	417	Lowest acceptable in the U.S.
9 carat	375	Common for UK jewelry
8 carat	333	Lowest acceptable in Europe
1 carat	41.7	Fundamental from which others are calculated

APPENDIX B

Frequently Asked Questions

How much gold is mined each year?
2,295 tons is projected to be mined in 2009 — the amount has been falling steadily over the last few years.

How much gold has ever been mined?
It is estimated that the amount of gold above ground is between 120,000 and 140,000 tons.

Which country produces the most gold?
In 2009 it is China, with 281.5 tons. South Africa led in 2006 with 272 tons, but it is projected to trail in third place in 2009 with 195.2 tons, behind Australia's 200.4 tons.

What is the world's most productive gold mine?
The Freegold Mine produced 115 tons of gold every year. The Driefontein Mine has produced more gold than any other mine, estimated at nearly 2,300 tons.

Where is the world's deepest gold mine?
AngloGold Ashanti's Mponeng in Carletonville, South Africa, is over 12,400 feet deep, and it is projected to go over 14,000 feet deep.

Which country uses the most gold?
In 2009, India will consume 320.8 tons of gold for jewelry alone.

What is most gold used for?
Jewelry. In 2009, 2,022.7 tons will be used.

APPENDIX C

Additional Resources

WEB SITES

Gold:

National Mining Association (NMA): **www.nma.org**

World Gold Council (WCG): **www.gold.org**

CPM Group: **www.cpmgroup.com**

Kitco: **www.kitco.com**

The Bullion Desk: **www.thebulliondesk.com**

Gold Anti-Trust Action Committee (GATA): **www.gata.org**

Gold Eagle: **www.gold-eagle.com**

Gold Fields Mineral Services (GFMS): **www.gfms.co.uk**

Gold Seek: **www.goldseek.com**

Gold Seeker: **www.gold-seeker.com**

321 Gold: **www.321gold.com**

American Gold Exchange: **www.amergold.com**

UtiliseGold: **www.utilisegold.com**

The Au Report: **www.theaureport.com**

Ton o Gold: **www.tonogold.com**

Wexford Capital Management: **www.wexfordcoin.com**

Silver:

The CPM Group: **www.cpmgroup.com**

The Silver Institute: **www.silverinstitute.org**

Kitco: **www.kitco.com**

New York Mercantile Exchange: **www.nymex.com**

SilverStrategies.com: **www.silverstrategies.com**

Silver-Investor: **www.silver-investor.com**

Silver Miners: **www.silverminers.com**

Silver Seek: **www.silverseek.com**

Platinum and palladium:

Metals Place: **www.metalsplace.com**

Platinum Today: **www.platinum.matthey.com**

Global Info Mine: **www.globalinfomine.com**

Stillwater Mining: **www.stillwatermining.com**

U.S. Geological Survey: **http://minerals.usgs.gov**

Uranium:

Investment U: **www.investmentu.com/uranium/html**

Prospect Uranium Inc.: **www.prospecturanium.com**

Uranium Seek: **www.uraniumseek.com**

U.S. Geological Survey: **http://minerals.usgs.gov**

Daily Reckoning: **www.dailyreckoning.com/uranium_rpt**

World Information Service on Energy: **www.wise-uranium.org**

World Nuclear Association: **www.world-nuclear.org**

Base metals:

U.S. Geological Survey: **http://minerals.usga.gov**

Base Metals: **www.basemetals.com**

Metal Prices: **www.metalprices.com**

Global Info Mine: **www.globalinfomine.com**

Additional Web sources:

American Stock Exchange: **www.amex.com**

ASX: **www.asx.com**

Bloomberg: **www.bloomberg.com**

Bullion Direct: **www.bulliondirect.com**

Bureau of Labor Statistics: **www.bls.gov**

Butler Research: **www.butlerresearch.com**

Canadian Insider: **www.canadianinsider.com**

Cincinnati Rare Coin Galleries: **www.mainstreetcoin.com**

Clive Maund: **www.clivemaund.com**

David W. Young: **www.goldsilverbullion.com**

Decision Point: **www.decisionpoint.com**

Daily Reckoning: **www.dailyreckoning.com**

Energy Information Administration (provides energy statistics for the U.S. government): **www.eia.doe.gov/fuelnuclear.html**

ETF Connect: **www.etfconnect.com**

Everbank: **www.everbank.com**

Financial Sense: **www.financialsense.com**

Future Source: **www.futuresource.com**

FX Street: **www.fxstreet.com**

Hard Assets Investor: **www.hardassetsinvestor.com**

How the Market Works: **www.howthemarketworks.com**

Inflation Data: **www.inflationdata.com**

Info Mine: **www.infomine.com**

International Monetary Fund: **www.imf.org**

Investment Rarities: **www.investmentrarities.com**

Kitco Casey: **www.kitcocasey.com**

LeMetropole Café: **www.lemetropolecafe.com**

Market Watch: **www.marketwatch.com**

Midwest Refineries: **www.midwestrefineries.com**

Mine Site: **www.minesite.com**

Mine Web: **www.mineweb.com**

Mineral Stox: **www.mineralstox.com**

Mining Sector Stocks: **www.miningsectorstocks.com**

Mining Weekly: **www.miningweekly.co.za**

National Mining Association (NMA): **www.nma.org**

Resource Investor: **www.resourceinvestor.com**

Shadow Stats: **www.shadowstats.com**

Speculative Investor: **www.speculative-investor.com**

Stock House: **www.stockhouse.com**

Stock Trak: **www.stocktrak.com**

TFC Commodity Charts: **www.futures.tradingcharts.com**

The Morgan Report: **www.TheMorganReport.com**

Trader Tracks: **www.tradertracks.com**

TSX: **www.tsx.com**

Yahoo! Finance: **http://finance.yahoo.com**

NEWSLETTERS

"Bullion Market Insights": **www.goldsilverbullion.com**

"Casey Research": **www.caseyresearch.com**

"Dow Theory Letters": **www.dowtheoryletters.com**

"Elliott Wave Theorist": **www.elliottwave.com**

"Forecast & Strategies": **www.mskousen.com**

"Free Gold Money Report": **www.fgmr.com**

"Gold Mining Stock Report": **www.goldminingstockreport.com**

"Gold Newsletter": **www.goldnewsletter.com**

"Gold Stock Analyst": **www.goldstockanalyst.com**

"Grant's Interest Rate Observer": **www.grantspub.com**

"International Harry Schultz Letter": **www.hsletter.com**

"J Taylor's Gold, Energy, & Tech Stocks Newsletter": **www.miningstocks.com**

"Le Metropole Café": **www.lemetropolecafe.com**

"Moneychanger": **www.the-moneychanger.com**

"Ormetal Report": **www.ormetal.com**

"Resource Opportunities": **www.resourceopportunities.com**

"The Aden Forecast": **www.adenforecast.com**

"The Dines Letter": **www.dinesletter.com**

"The Ruff Times:" **www.rufftimes.com**

GLOSSARY OF TERMS

Accelerated supply — Gold that has not been produced yet that is marketed in advance through hedging or other financial contracts.

Allocated account — Opened when the customer requires specific gold or other precious metal to be segregated from other customers holdings.

Alloy — A mixture of two or more elements, in the case of gold to make it more durable for jewelry. Reduces the purity.

American style option — As described in this book, this type of option can be exercised at any time before the expiration date. Contrast to the European style option.

Arbitrage — A trading technique that involves simultaneously buying and selling the same asset, usually in different markets, to capitalize on slightly different prices.

Ask — The price that a dealer wants for a commodity or security.

Assay — The testing of material to determine metal type and concentration of metal content.

Assay mark — The stamp made by an assayer on an ingot to guarantee its content.

At-the-money option — An option that is at the current market price.

Backwardation — Refers to the spot price being more than the forward price in the market; the opposite of contango.

Base metals — These include copper, aluminum, lead, zinc, tin, and nickel. Base metals have a number of industrial and monetary uses.

Bear market — A period during which prices in the market are generally falling. Investors tend to sell commodities during a bear market to minimize loss.

Bid — The price that a dealer will pay for a commodity or security.

Binary options — A form of option contract that pays out all or nothing, depending whether the commodity price meets a limit value.

Blank — A disc of metal that is stamped to become a coin.

Bond — A form of debt, a company or government will issue a bond for investors to buy with the promise of repayment later with interest.

Broker — A person who acts as a mediator between a buyer and a seller.

Brokerage firm — A business that acts as a broker on behalf of its clients.

Bull market — A period during which the market is rising. Investors tend to buy commodities during bull markets to make a profit.

Bullion — Precious metals in the form of bars, wafers, ingots, or coins that are not numismatic.

Call option — A contract giving a buyer the right but not the obligation to purchase a security or commodity at a certain price on or before a certain date.

Carat — A measure of the purity of gold on the basis that 24 carats is pure gold. Also used as a measurement for the weight of precious gems.

CBOT — The Chicago Board of Trade.

Central banks — The body responsible for setting monetary policy for a group of states or a country.

CFTC — The Commodity Futures Trading Commission, which regulates futures and options.

COMEX — New York Mercantile Exchange; the world's largest commodity futures exchange.

Commemorative coins — Coins minted to mark an important person or significant event.

Commission — Usually a percentage; money paid to a broker or other agent for services.

Commodity — Any good or service that has a demand.

Contango — A situation where the forward price is more than the spot price for a commodity or security, and the opposite of backwardation.

Coupon — A term for the interest associated with a bond issue.

Covered call option — The writer of the call option already owns the underlying asset, which may be "called away" by the buyer of the option.

Currency — A store of value that is used in exchange for goods and services.

Derivative — A financial instrument that is based on an under-lying security, but which does not directly involve ownership of the security.

Diversify — To invest in a variety of commodities and/or use a number of vehicles to minimize risk and potentially see greater appreciation.

ETF — Exchange-traded fund.

European style option — The type of option offered in European markets can only be exercised on the actual date of expiry, and not at any time before as with the American version.

Exercising — Referring to options, it is when the buyer of the option requires fulfillment of the contract.

Expiration date — The last day on which an option can be exercised.

Exploratory mine — A new mine that is attempting to find its chosen commodity.

FDIC — Federal Deposit Insurance Corporation; generally guarantees up to $250,000 per individual investor for checking and savings accounts.

Fiat currency — Paper money printed by a nation's government designed to pay for goods and services.

Fineness — The amount of precious metal in an alloy, expressed as parts per thousand.

Fool's gold — Iron pyrites, which are shiny and yellow, and can be mistaken for gold by amateur prospectors.

Fundamental analysis — A study of the financials of a company or a commodity, usually to determine the long-term prospects for the price.

Futures contract — A contract for a specified commodity or financial security to be delivered on a set date in the future at a set price.

Gold — A bright yellow precious metal; symbol Au.

Gold standard — Guaranteeing the value of paper money with the value of gold.

Gold/Silver ratio — The number of ounces of silver that can be bought with 1 ounce of gold.

Hallmark — Marks on gold or silver that indicate the quality of the item.

Hedging — A financial strategy that involves buying different financial instruments to offset the risk of an adverse movement in price.

IMF — International Monetary Fund.

In-the-money option — An option that has become profitable. For a call option, when the strike price of the option is less than the current market price, and for a put option, when the strike price of the option is more than the current market price.

Inflation — A rise in the price of goods or services over a period of time.

Ingot — Metal cast into a shape that makes it easier to mold into the desired product.

Intrinsic value — Referring to options, this is the difference between the strike price and the current market price.

Investment — Relating to personal finances, this is the purchase of a commodity for the purpose of realizing capital gains, although losses may be incurred.

IRA (traditional or Roth) — Individual retirement arrangement; retirement plans that offer tax savings.

Liquidity — The amount of trading or turnover in a market, which gives an indication of how easy it is to liquidate, or sell, your position if you want to.

Long — To be long a commodity, share, or contract means that you are a buyer. Compare with short.

Margin — Cash deposit you are expected to pay to your broker to cover credit risk.

Maturity date — Also known as an expiration date, this is the date for an option to expire, whether or not it is in the money.

Mid-tier mine — A newer mine that has a reputation for producing its chosen commodity.

Naked option — An option that has not been hedged and is exposed to be exercised at the full cost.

Numismatic coins — Collectible coins that are valuable because of collectibility, in addition to precious metal content.

NYMEX — New York Mercantile Exchange; the world's largest commodity futures exchange.

Offer — The price at which a dealer is willing to sell.

Option — A contract that stipulates the ability to buy or sell a commodity at a specified value at a specific time.

OTC — Over-the-counter; a term used for financial securities that are not traded through exchange.

Out-of-the-money option — An option that has no intrinsic value. For a call option, the strike price is greater than the market price, and with a put option, the strike price is less than the commodity is available for on the open market. If such an option occurs on the expiration date, then it expires worthless.

Palladium — Whitish-silver metal, symbol Pd.

Platinum — Grayish-white element, symbol Pt.

Portfolio — The investments of a person of business (e.g., stock portfolio).

Premium — Additional cost paid by the buyer for the privilege of buying the security or commodity.

Principal to principal — Transactions that occur directly between the buyer and seller without involving an exchange.

Put option — A contract giving the buyer the option to sell a security for a specified price any time during the option.

Refining — Separating and purifying precious metals from contaminants.

Scrap gold — Refers to any gold that is sent back to a refiner or processor to be recycled.

Silver — Shiny, white metal, symbol Ag.

Short — In trading, to be short means that you have sold the security or commodity without owning it, and are required to buy and replace it later. Borrowing the security that is sold is taken care of by your broker. *See a full description in the trading section in Chapter Six.*

Smelting — Melting ore to separate the metal content from impurities.

Speculating — Making an educated guess about where the market is headed.

Spot market — The current market for immediate delivery, hence spot price is the current market price for a commodity.

Stock market — A system where bids are placed on the stocks and stock derivatives of companies.

Strike price — The agreed price in an option contract at which the contract may be fulfilled

The Fed — The Federal Reserve; the central bank of the United States.

Swap — Selling a commodity with a simultaneous buying of a forward contract for the same amount.

Time value — Referring to options, and the length of time until expiration; time value is the additional value or cost associated with that time.

Top-tier mine — A mine that has a reputation for producing its chosen commodity.

Trading — Buying and selling commodities to make a profit, either short-term or long-term.

Unallocated account — An account where the customer has a general entitlement to the stored metal, but without particular bars being assigned. A simple and cheap way of holding metal, although the customer is an unsecured creditor in the event of bankruptcy.

Underlying — When trading in derivatives such as options and futures, the underlying is the stock or commodity on which the trade is based.

Uranium — A chemical element with important military and energy uses; symbol U.

Volatility — The amount of change in price of the financial instrument.

Writing options — Taking the position of the option seller, and giving the buyer the option to buy or sell a commodity or financial instrument at a set price before an expiration date.

BIBLIOGRAPHY

Cochran, K. *Junior Mining Investor: 14 Natural Resource Experts Show You How To Invest Profitably in Emerging Gold, Silver, Platinum, Base Metals, and Uranium Mining and Exploration Stocks.* Bang Printing, United States of America (2007).

Dunwiddie, Alan. *How to Invest in Gold and Silver.* Ad Publishing (2008).

Duncan, Richard. *The Dollar Crisis: Causes, Consequences, Cures.* Wiley (2005). This hardcover book relies on the advice of a International Monetary Fund (IMF) consultant to explain in detail why the dollar will collapse in the coming years.

Katz, John and Holmes, Frank. *The Goldwatcher: Demystifying Gold Investing.* John Wiley & Sons (2008).

Kindleberger, Charles P. *Manias, Panics, and Crashes: A History of Financial Crisis.* This hardcover book provides historical and theoretical information about why the world continues to experience financial problems.

Kosares, M. *The ABCs of Gold Investing: How to Protect and Build Your Wealth with Gold.* Addicus Books, Omaha, NE (2005).

Lips, Ferdinand. *Gold Wars: The Battle Against Sound Money as Seen from a Swiss Perspective.* Fame (2002). This handy paperback book was written by a Swiss economist, and it explains the abandonment of the concept of gold as money as well as central banks' ongoing attempts to manipulate gold prices.

MacKay, Charles. *Extraordinary Popular Delusions & the Madness of Crowds.* Three Rivers Press (1995). This hardcover book covers historical financial bubbles.

Maloney, Michael. *Guide to Investing in Gold & Silver: Protect Your Financial Future.* Business Plus (2008).

McGuire, S. *Buy Gold Now: How a Real Estate Bust, Our Bulging National Debt, and Languishing Dollar will Push Gold to Record Highs.* John Wiley & Sons, Inc., Hoboken, NJ (2008).

Mladjenovic, P. *Precious Metals Investing for Dummies.* Wiley Publishing, Inc., Indianapolis, IN (2008).

Morgan, D. *Get the Skinny on: Silver Investing.* Morgan James Publishing, Garden City, NY (2006).

Partnoy, Frank. *Infectious Greed: How Deceit and Risk Corrupted the Financial Markets.* Profile Business (2004). This paperback book explains how derivatives corrupt global capitalism.

Rothbard, Murray. *The Case for the 100 percent Gold Dollar* and *What Has Government Done to our Money?* Ludwig von Mises Institute (2005). These two books are libertarian in nature, and the author seeks to examine the nature of money and the future of gold in the monetary system.

Ruff. H. *Ruff's Little Book of Big Fortunes in Gold & Silver: A Middle Class License to Print Money*. 10 Finger Press, Soquel, CA (2006).

Spall, Jonathan. *Investing in Gold*. McGraw Hill (2009).

Stathis, Mike. *America's Financial Apocalypse: How to Profit from the Next Great Depression*. AVA Publishing (2006).

Turk, J., and Rubino, J. *The Collapse of the Dollar and How to Profit from it: Make a Fortune by Investing in Gold and Other Hard Assets*. Doubleday, New York, NY (2004).

von Mises, Ludwig. *The Theory of Money & Credit* and *Human Action*. Lassez Faire Books (2008). Both of these books are economic texts, but the work of this well respected founding Austrian economist is worth a look.

Weldon. G. *Gold Trading Boot Camp: How to Master the Basics and Become a Successful Commodities Investor*. John Wiley & Sons, Inc., Hoboken, NJ (2008).

AUTHOR BIOGRAPHY

Alan Northcott is a successful financial author, freelance writer, trader,
professional engineer, farmer, kara-
oke jockey, and wedding officiant,
along with other pursuits. He and his
wife now live in Colorado, having
moved recently from the Midwest.

Originating from England, he immi-
grated with his wife to America in
1992. His engineering career spanned
more than 30 years on both sides of the Atlantic, and recent years
have found him seeking and living a more diverse, fulfilling life-
style. This is the sixth financial book he has written, and the previous works are also available from Atlantic Publishing.

He offers a free newsletter on various related topics. You can find
out more at **www.alannorthcott.com**, or e-mail him directly at
alannorthcott@msn.com.

INDEX

R

S

T

U

V

W

Z